STEP-BY-STEP
Low Fat Cookbook

STEP-BY-STEP
Low Fat Cookbook

Catherine Atkinson

Photographs by James Duncan

SMITHMARK

© Anness Publishing Limited 1995

This edition published in 1995 by
SMITHMARK Publishers Inc.
16 East 32nd Street
New York
NY 10016

SMITHMARK books are available for bulk purchase for sales
promotion and for premium use. For details write or call
the Manager of Special Sales, SMITHMARK Publishers Inc.
16 East 32nd Street, New York, NY, 10016; (212) 532–6600.

ISBN 0-8317-6549-6

Produced by Anness Publishing Limited
1 Boundary Row
London SE1 8HP

Editorial Director: Joanna Lorenz
Series Editor: Lindsay Porter
Designer: Peter Laws
Jacket Designer: Peter Butler
Photographer: James Duncan
Stylist: Madeleine Brehaut

Typeset by MC Typeset Ltd, Rochester, Kent
Printed and bound in Hong Kong

Note: Nutritional information is provided per portion for
all recipes. Where a recipe serves, for example,
4-6, the information is based on the larger portion.

CONTENTS

INTRODUCTION

So much has been written in the past decade about what we should and shouldn't eat, it's hardly surprising we're sceptical about dietary advice – it seems that everything we enjoy is bad for us. Often nutritionists are vague and simply suggest eating 'a balanced diet'. However, when it comes to avoiding heart disease, recommendations are loud and clear: reduce your intake of fat (especially saturated) and you'll considerably reduce the risk of heart disease.

But what does this mean when you're shopping at the supermarket, faced with confusingly labeled foods? What exactly is saturated fat and how do we begin to limit the amount of fat we eat? These are the questions that are answered in this book.

Cutting down on fat doesn't mean sacrificing taste. It's easy to follow a healthy eating plan without becoming a fanatic. There's no need to forgo all your favorite foods, as the recipes in this book illustrate, but you may have to alter your approach to cooking and choose ingredients that are naturally lower in fat and prepare them with little – if any – additional fat. This is not as limiting as it sounds – you can still enjoy hearty main courses and desserts so delicious it's hard to believe they're good for you. With this in mind, it won't be long before you develop a preference for lower fat versions of everyday foods.

Facts about Fats

It's important to know something about different fats before we can make changes to the way we eat – some fats are believed to be less harmful than others.

Fats in our foods are made up of building blocks of fatty acids and glycerol and their properties vary according to each combination. There are three main types of fatty acids; saturated, polyunsaturated and unsaturated or mono-unsaturated. There is always a combination of each of the three types in any food, but the amount of each type varies greatly from one food to another.

SATURATED FATS

All fatty acids are made up of chains of carbon atoms. Each atom has one or more free 'bonds' to link with other atoms and by doing so the fatty acid transports nutrients to cells throughout the body. Without these free 'bonds' the atom cannot form any links, that is to say, it's completely 'saturated'. Because of this, the body finds it hard to process the fatty acid into energy, so simply stores it as fat.

The main type of saturated fat is found in food of animal origin – meat and dairy products such as lard and butter, which are solid at room temperature. However, there are also some saturated fats of vegetable origin, notably coconut and palm oils. A few margarines and oils are processed by changing some of the unsaturated fatty acids to saturated ones; these are labelled 'hydrogenated vegetable oil' and should be avoided.

MONOUNSATURATED FATS

These are found in foods such as olive oil, rapeseed oil (canola), some nuts, oily fish and avocados. They may help lower the blood cholesterol and this could explain why in Mediterranean countries there is such a low incidence of heart disease.

Above: *Some oils such as olive and rapeseed (canola) are thought to help lower blood cholesterol.*

Above left: *Animal products such as lard and butter and some margarines are major sources of saturated fats.*

Right: *Vegetable and plant oils and some margarines are high in polyunsaturated fat.*

POLYUNSATURATED FATS

There are two types, those of vegetable or plant origin, such as sunflower oil, soft margarine and seeds (omega 6) and those from oily fish (omega 3). Both are usually liquid at room temperature.

At one time it was believed to be beneficial to switch to polyunsaturates as they may also help lower cholesterol. Today most experts believe that it's more important to reduce the total intake of all kinds of fat.

The Cholesterol Question

Cholesterol is a fat-like substance which plays a vital role in the body. It's the material from which many essential hormones and vitamin D are made. However, too much saturated fat encourages the body to make more cholesterol than it needs or can get rid of.

Cholesterol is carried around the body, attached to proteins called high density lipoproteins (HDL), low density lipoproteins (LDL), and very low density lipoproteins (VLDL or triglycerides). After eating, the LDLs carry the fat in the blood to the cells where it's required. Any surplus should be excreted from the body; however, if there is too much LDL in the blood, some of the fat will be deposited on the walls of the arteries. This scaling up gradually narrows the arteries and is one of the most common causes of heart attacks and strokes. In contrast, HDLs appear to protect against heart disease. Whether high triglyceride levels are risk factors remains unknown.

For some people, an excess of cholesterol in the blood is a hereditary trait; in others, it's mainly due to the consumption of too much saturated fat. In both cases though, it can be reduced by a low fat diet. Many people believe naturally high cholesterol foods such as egg yolks and organ meats should be avoided, but research has shown that it is more important to reduce total fat intake.

FATS & OILS		
Saturated	**Monounsaturated**	**Polyunsaturated**
Butter	Olive oil	Corn oil
Lard	Grapeseed oil	Safflower oil
Hard margarine	Rapeseed (Canola) oil	Soybean oil
Suet		Sunflower oil
Vegetarian suet		Walnut oil
Coconut oil		Soft margarines, labelled 'high in polyunsaturates'
Palm oil		

Planning a Low Fat Diet

Most of us eat about 4 oz of fat everyday. Yet just ¼ oz – that's about the amount in a single package of chips or a thin slice of Cheddar cheese – is all we need.

Current nutritional advice isn't quite that strict though and suggests that we should limit our daily intake to no more than 30% of total calories. In real terms, this means that for an average intake of 2000 calories a day, 30% of energy would come from 600 calories. Since each gram of fat provides 9 calories, your total daily intake should be no more than 66.6 g fat. If you look at page 11 you'll see how easy it is to consume this amount.

It's easy to cut down on obvious sources of fat such as butter, margarine, cream, whole milk and high fat cheeses, but watch out for hidden fats in food. We tend to think of cakes and biscuits as sweet foods, but usually more calories come from their fat content than from the sugar. Fat makes up about half the weight of nuts and even the leanest red meat, completely trimmed of all visible fat, still contains about 10% fat. About one-quarter of the fat we eat comes from meat and meat products, one-fifth from dairy products and margarine and the rest from cakes, cookies, pastries and other foods.

Butter vs Margarine

Butter and margarine producers have spent thousands on advertising, trying to convince us that their product is the healthiest. Both butter and margarine contain 80% fat and the same number of calories (737 Kcals in 3½ oz). Butter, however, is high in saturated fat. Margarine may also contain a high proportion of saturated fat, or it may be a type that is high in polyunsaturates, so it's important to check the label.

Low fat spreads and half fat or reduced fat butters contain 40% fat; the rest is water and milk solids emulsified together. There are also very low fat spreads around, containing 20–30% fat. Some are less palatable than others, so it's worth trying several to find one you like the taste of!

Labeling

Look at labels when choosing food. Ingredients are listed in order of quantity, so watch out for those with fat near the top. Nutritional labels can be misleading if you don't understand what they mean.

Low fat
Contains less than half the fat of the standard product. Remember that some foods are very high in fat. Think twice about buying 'low fat' sausages or chips.

Reduced fat
Contains less than 75% of the fat of the standard product.

Low cholesterol
No more than 0.005% of the total fat is cholesterol.

High in polyunsaturates/low in saturates
Contains at least 35% fat of which at least 45% of the fatty acids are polyunsaturated and not more than 25% saturated.

The Lowdown on Low Fat

Reduce your fat intake simply by switching to lower fat foods.

0.2 g fat
1 tsp whole milk
scant 1 cup skim milk

1.0 g fat
½ cup low fat plain yogurt
½ oz strained whole yogurt
1 thin slice (¹⁄₂₀th) avocado pear
3 bananas
9 apples, apricots, peaches, pears, oranges or small bunches of grapes

2.5 g fat
1 small pork bacon rasher
8 turkey bacon rashers

10 g fat
½ cup reduced fat cocoa powder
¼ cup cocoa powder

12 g fat
½ oz butter
1 oz low fat spread

15 g fat
2 oz Cheddar cheese
2½ oz Edam cheese
3 oz feta cheese
4 oz reduced fat cheddar
7 oz cottage cheese

WEIGHING NOTE
The weights given here have been rounded slightly up or down to make measuring portions easier.

Choosing Foods

The amount of fat, particularly saturated fat, is affected by two main factors – the type of foods we eat most often and the way in which we prepare and cook them.

Low fat doesn't mean no fat. It's misleading to start thinking simply of 'good' and 'bad' foods, it's really how much we eat of them that matters.

If you are going to cut down your fat intake, you'll need to make other alterations to your diet to compensate. High-fiber fruit, vegetables and cereals will help fill the gap. You should aim to increase your intake of carbohydrate foods to provide more than half your energy requirements. This will not only make your diet healthier, but you will also gradually lose weight, if you need to.

contain no more than 10% milk fat, although many are fat-free. Reduced fat cream cheese has 10–20% milk fat. By comparison, cream cheese has more than 45% milk fat, so a switch to any of the others is a good move.

MEAT AND FISH

Always trim meat of any visible fat and skim stocks and casseroles (this is easiest if you cool them first) Buy lean bacon rather than regular bacon and cut all the fat off before cooking. The red meats – lamb, pork and beef – are the highest in saturated fats, so try to eat chicken and turkey more often, but always remove the skin, which is high in fat. Avoid meat products such as sausages, salami and pâtés which are very high in fat.

Fish has a lower fat content than meat, and fish oils may help reduce blood cholesterol levels, although this remains unproven. Certainly, fish oils make blood clotting less likely to occur and as clots are an important factor in causing heart attacks, consumption of fish may be beneficial.

MILK, YOGURT AND CREAM

The fat content of ordinary milk is not particularly high – 3.9 g per ½ cup of milk – but you may consume quite a lot in tea, coffee or cooking. If you drink 2 cups of milk a day, you'll be adding about 20 g of fat to your intake. It's therefore worth switching to skim milk, which has virtually all the fat content removed, or at least to low fat milk. Beware of dried skim milk and coffee creamers – these may be skimmed of animal fat, but may have vegetable fat added.

Yogurt allows low fat foodies to enjoy many dishes that would otherwise be denied to them because of their cream content. Low fat natural yogurt has less than 2% fat, but if you need a thicker product for cooking, strain off some of the whey (see page 21), or drain the yogurt thoroughly. It will reduce by about half and make an excellent substitute for heavy cream or cream cheese.

Reduced fat versions of light, heavy and whipping creams are also available; but don't be too lavish with them as they're still fairly high in fat.

CHEESE

One-third of hard cheese is fat. Even Continental cheeses such as Edam contain about one-fifth fat. It is, however, a useful flavoring ingredient in cooking if used sparingly. Choose a strongly-flavored cheese like mature Cheddar or Parmesan and you'll need a lot less. There are also reduced fat alternatives to Cheddar and Cheshire which contain about half the fat of their full fat counterparts. These are good for 'eating', but are less successful for cooking.

Low fat cream or cottage cheese is an excellent substitute for cream cheese. Look out too for 'quark' and various cheeses which may be simply labelled as 'reduced fat cheese' or 'low fat cream cheese'. By definition, a low fat cheese must

Easy Ways to Cut Down Fat and Saturated Fat

EAT LESS

TRY INSTEAD

Butter and hard fats.

Try spreading butter more thinly, or replace it with a low fat spread or polyunsaturated margarine.

Fatty meats and high fat products such as meat pies and sausages.

Buy the leanest cuts of meat you can afford and choose low fat meats like skinless chicken or turkey. Look for reduced fat sausages and meat products. Eat fish more often, especially oily fish.

Full fat dairy products like cream, butter, hard margarine, milk and hard cheeses.

Choose skim or 1% low fat milk and milk products, and try low fat yogurt, low fat fromage frais and lower fat cheeses such as skim milk cream cheese, reduced fat Cheddar, mozzarella or Brie.

Hard cooking fats such as lard or hard margarine.

Choose monounsaturated or polyunsaturated oils for cooking, such as olive, sunflower, corn or soybean oil.

Rich salad dressings like mayonnaise or cream dressing.

Make salad dressings with low fat yogurt or fromage frais, or use a healthy oil such as olive oil.

Fried foods.

Broil, microwave, steam or bake when possible. Roast meats on a rack. Fill up on starchy foods like pasta, rice and couscous. Choose baked or boiled potatoes, not fried.

Added fat in cooking.

Use heavy-based or non-stick pans so you can cook with little or no added fat.

High fat snacks such as chips, chocolate, cakes, pastries and cookies.

Choose fresh or dried fruit, breadsticks or vegetable sticks. Make your own low fat cakes and bakes.

The Fat and Calorie Contents of Food

The following figures show the weight of fat (g) and the energy content per 4 oz of each food.

VEGETABLES	Fat (g)	Energy
Broccoli	0.9	33 Kcals
Cabbage	0.4	26 K/cals
Cauliflower	0.9	34 Kcals
Carrots	0.3	35 Kcals
Cucumber	0.1	10 Kcals
Mushrooms	0.5	13 Kcals
Onions	0.2	36 Kcals
Peas	1.5	83 Kcals
Potatoes	0.2	75 Kcals
French fries, homemade	6.7	189 Kcals
French fries, retail	12.4	239 Kcals
French fries, frozen, baked	4.2	163 Kcals
Tomatoes	0.3	17 Kcals
Zucchini	0.4	18 Kcals
Chick-peas, whole, dried	5.4	320 Kcals
Hummus	12.6	187 Kcals
Red kidney beans, dried	1.1	279 Kcals

Information from **The Composition of Foods**, 5th Edition, (1991) is reproduced with the permission of the Royal Society of Chemistry and the Controller of Her Majesty's Stationery Office.

FISH	Fat (g)	Energy
Cod fillets, raw	0.7	76 Kcals
Cod in batter, fried in oil	10.3	199 Kcals
Crab, canned	0.9	81 Kcals
Haddock, raw	0.6	73 Kcals
Lemon sole, raw	1.4	81 Kcals
Shrimp	1.8	107 Kcals
Trout, steamed	4.5	135 Kcals

MEAT PRODUCTS	Fat (g)	Energy
Bacon rasher	39.5	414 Kcals
Turkey bacon rasher	1.0	99 K/cals
Beef, ground, raw	16.2	221 Kcals
Sirloin steak, lean and fat	12.1	218 Kcals
Sirloin steak, lean only	6.0	168 Kcals
Lamb chops, loin, lean and fat	29.0	355 Kcals
Lamb chops, loin, lean only	12.3	122 Kcals
Pork chops, loin, lean and fat	24.2	332 Kcals
Pork chops, loin, lean only	10.7	226 Kcals
Chicken fillet, raw	2.7	109 Kcals
Chicken fillet, breaded, fried oil	12.7	242 Kcals
Duck, meat only, raw	4.8	122 Kcals
Duck, roasted, meat, fat and skin	29.0	339 Kcals
Turkey, meat only, raw	2.2	107 Kcals
Liver, lamb, raw	10.3	179 Kcals
Pork pie	27.0	376 Kcals
Salami	45.2	491 Kcals

DAIRY, FATS & OILS	Fat (g)	Energy
Cream, heavy	48.0	449 Kcals
Cream, light	19.1	198 K/cals
Cream, whipping	39.3	373 Kcals
Milk, skim	0.1	33 Kcals
Milk, whole	3.9	66 Kcals
Brie	26.9	319 Kcals
Cheddar cheese	34.4	412 Kcals
Cheddar-type, reduced fat	15.0	261 Kcals
Cream cheese	47.4	439 Kcals
Edam cheese	25.4	333 Kcals
Feta cheese	20.2	250 Kcals
Parmesan cheese	32.7	452 Kcals
Low fat yogurt, plain	0.8	56 Kcals
Whole yogurt	9.1	115 Kcals
Butter	81.7	737 Kcals
Margarine	81.6	739 Kcals
Low fat spread	40.5	390 Kcals
Lard	99.0	891 Kcals
Coconut oil	99.9	899 Kcals
Corn oil	99.9	899 Kcals
Olive oil	99.9	899 Kcals
Safflower oil	99.9	899 Kcals
Eggs (about 2)	10.9	147 Kcals
Egg yolk	30.5	339 Kcals
Egg white	Trace	36 Kcals

CEREALS, BAKING & PRESERVES	Fat (g)	Energy
Brown rice, uncooked	2.8	357 Kcals
White rice, uncooked	3.6	383 K/cals
Pasta, white, uncooked	1.8	342 Kcals
Brown bread	2.0	218 Kcals
Croissant	20.3	360 Kcals
Pancake	26.6	484 Kcals
Shortbread	26.1	498 Kcals
Digestive biscuit (plain)	20.9	471 Kcals
Madeira cake	16.9	393 Kcals
Angelfood	6.1	294 Kcals
Sugar, white	0	394 Kcals
Chocolate, milk	30.3	529 Kcals
Honey	0	288 Kcals
Lemon Curd	5.i	283 Kcals
Fruit jam	0	261 Kcals
Marmalade	0	261 Kcals

FRUIT & NUTS	Fat (g)	Energy
Apples, eating	0.1	47 Kcals
Avocados	19.5	190 Kcals
Bananas	0.3	95 Kcals
Dried mixed fruit	1.6	227 Kcals
Grapefruit	0.1	30 Kcals
Oranges	0.1	37 Kcals
Peaches	0.1	33 Kcals
Almonds	55.8	612 Kcals
Brazil nuts	68.2	682 Kcals
Pine nuts	68.6	688 Kcals
Peanut butter, smooth	53.7	623 Kcals

Equipment

There are only a few essentials for low fat recipes – accurate measuring and weighing equipment and a non-stick frying pan. There are, however, many gadgets which make cooking with the minimum of fat a lot easier.

Baking sheet
A flat, rigid, non-stick baking sheet ensures even cooking.

Baking tray
A shallow-sided non-stick tray that won't buckle at high temperatures is ideal for roasting.

Bowls
A set of bowls is useful for mixing, whisking and soaking. A non-porous material such as glass or stainless steel is essential when whisking egg whites.

Chopping board
A hygienic nylon board is recommended for chopping and cutting.

Colander
This is useful for draining cooked pasta and vegetables quickly.

Cook's knife
A large all-purpose cook's knife is essential for chopping, dicing and slicing.

Filleting knife
A thin, flexible-bladed knife is useful for filleting fish.

Frying pan
A non-stick surface is vital for 'frying' and browning meat and vegetables.

Large spoon
Use this for folding in, stirring and basting.

Measuring cups or weighing scales
Use these for accurately measuring both dry and wet ingredients.

Measuring spoons
Essential for measuring small quantities accurately.

Non-stick coated fabric sheet
This re-usable non-stick material can be cut to size, and used to line cake pans, baking sheets or frying pans. Heat resistant up to 550°F and microwave-safe, it will last up to 5 years.

Non-stick baking paper
Ideal for lining cake pans and baking sheets without the need for greasing.

Non-stick baking tins
For easy removal of low fat bakes and sponge cakes.

Perforated spoon
Useful for lifting cooked food out of cooking liquid.

Ridged broiling pan
For giving broiled meat and vegetables characteristic 'grill marks'.

Sieve
For sifting dry ingredients and draining yogurt.

Small grater
For finely grating fresh Parmesan cheese and nutmeg.

Vegetable peeler
For preparing fruit and vegetables.

Whisk
Essential for whisking egg whites and for thorough mixing.

non-stick baking paper

non-stick baking pans

ridged broiling pan

non-stick baking pans

non-stick coated fabric sheet

sieve

large spoon

measuring spoons

baking sheet

chopping boards

vegetable peeler

Chicken Stock

This classic, flavorful stock forms the base for many soups and sauces.

Makes 6¹/₄ cups

INGREDIENTS
2¹/₄ lb chicken wings or thighs
1 onion
2 whole cloves
1 bay leaf
1 sprig of thyme
3–4 sprigs of parsley
10 black peppercorns

Vegetable Stock

A vegetarian version of the basic stock.

Makes 6¹/₄ cups

INGREDIENTS
2 carrots
2 celery stalks
2 onions
2 tomatoes
10 mushroom stems
2 bay leaves
1 sprig of thyme
3–4 sprigs of parsley
10 black peppercorns

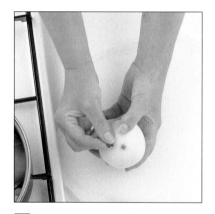

1 Cut the chicken into pieces and put into a large, heavy-based saucepan. Peel the onion and stick with the cloves. Tie the bay leaf, thyme, parsley and peppercorns in a piece of cheesecloth and add to the saucepan with the onion.

2 Pour in 7½ cups of cold water. Slowly bring to simmering point, skimming off any scum which rises to the surface with a slotted spoon. Continue to simmer very gently, uncovered, for 1½ hours.

1 Roughly chop the carrots, celery, onions, tomatoes and mushroom stems. Place them in a large heavy-based saucepan. Tie the bay leaves, thyme, parsley and peppercorns in a piece of cheesecloth and add to the pan.

2 Pour in 7½ cups cold water. Slowly bring to simmering point. Continue to simmer very gently, uncovered, for 1½ hours.

3 Strain the stock through a sieve into a large bowl and leave until cold. Remove any fat from the surface with a slotted spoon. Keep chilled in the refrigerator until required, or freeze in usable amounts.

3 Strain through a sieve into a large bowl and leave until cold. Keep chilled in the refrigerator until required, or freeze in usable amounts.

Peeling and Seeding Tomatoes

This is an efficient way of preparing tomatoes.

1 Use a sharp knife to cut a small cross on the bottom of the tomato.

2 Turn the tomato over and cut out the core.

3 Immerse the tomato in boiling water for 10–15 seconds, then transfer to a bowl of cold water using a slotted spoon.

4 Lift out the tomato and peel (the skin should be easy to remove).

5 Cut the tomato in half crosswise and squeeze out the seeds.

6 Use a large knife to cut the peeled tomato into strips, then chop across the strips to make dice.

Sautéed Onions

Fried onions form the basis of many savory recipes. This is a fat free version.

INGREDIENTS
2 medium onions, sliced
¾ cup chicken or vegetable
   stock
1 tbsp dry red or white wine or wine
   vinegar

1 Put the onions and stock into a non-stick frying pan. Cover and bring to the boil. Simmer for 1 minute.

2 Uncover and boil for about 5 minutes, or until the stock has reduced entirely. Lower the heat and stir the onions until just beginning to color.

3 Add the wine or vinegar and continue to cook until the onions are dry and lightly browned.

Whipped 'Cream'

Serve this sweet 'cream' instead of whipped heavy cream. It isn't suitable for cooking, but freezes very well.

Makes ⅔ cup

INGREDIENTS
½ tsp powdered gelatin
¼ cup non fat milk
   powder
1 tbsp superfine sugar
1 tbsp lemon juice

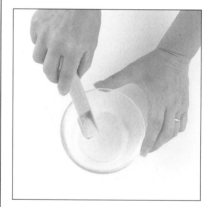 

1 Sprinkle the gelatin over 1 tbsp cold water in a small bowl and leave to 'sponge' for 5 minutes. Place the bowl over a saucepan of hot water and stir until dissolved. Leave to cool.

2 Whisk the skim milk powder, superfine sugar, lemon juice and 4 tbsp cold water until frothy. Add the dissolved gelatin and whisk for a few seconds more. Chill in the refrigerator for 30 minutes.

3 Whisk the chilled mixture again until very thick and frothy. Serve within 30 minutes of making.

Strained Yogurt and Simple Cottage Cheese

Strained yogurt and cottage cheese are simple to make at home, and tend to be lower in fat than commercial varieties. Serve strained yogurt with desserts instead of cream, sweetened with a little honey, if liked. Cottage cheese can be used instead of sour cream, cream cheese or butter, flavored with chopped herbs.

Makes 1¼ cups of strained yogurt or ½ cup cottage cheese

INGREDIENTS
2½ cups plain low fat
    yogurt

1 Line a nylon or stainless steel sieve with a double layer of cheesecloth. Put over a bowl and pour in the yogurt.

2 Leave to drain in the refrigerator for 3 hours – it will have separated into thick strained yogurt and watery whey.

3 For cottage cheese, leave to drain in the refrigerator for 8 hours or overnight. Spoon the curd cheese into a bowl, cover and keep chilled until required.

Yogurt Piping Cream

This is an excellent alternative to whipped cream for decorating cakes and desserts.

Makes scant 2 cups

INGREDIENTS
2 tsp powdered gelatin
1¼ cups strained yogurt
1 tbsp fructose
½ tsp vanilla extract
1 egg white

1 Sprinkle the gelatin over 3 tbsp cold water in a small bowl and leave to 'sponge' for 5 minutes. Place the bowl over a saucepan of hot water and stir until dissolved. Leave to cool.

2 Mix together the yogurt, fructose and vanilla extract. Stir in the gelatin. Chill in the refrigerator for 30 minutes, or until just beginning to set around the edges.

3 Whisk the egg white until stiff and carefully fold it into the yogurt mixture. Spoon into a piping bag fitted with a piping nozzle and use immediately.

Roasted Pepper Soup

Broiling intensifies the flavor of sweet red and yellow bell peppers and helps this soup keep its stunning color.

Serves 4

INGREDIENTS
3 red bell peppers
1 yellow bell pepper
1 medium onion, chopped
1 garlic clove, crushed
3⅔ cups vegetable
   stock
1 tbsp flour
salt and freshly ground black pepper
red and yellow bell peppers, diced, to
   garnish

peppers

flour

stock

onion

NUTRITIONAL NOTES

PER SERVING:

CALORIES 66 **PROTEIN** 2.26 g
FAT 0.72 g **SATURATED FAT** 0
CARBOHYDRATE 13.40 g **FIBER** 2.54 g
ADDED SUGAR 0 **SODIUM** 0.01 g

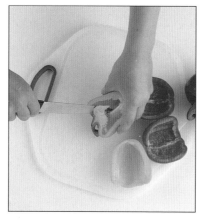

1 Preheat the broiler. Halve the peppers and cut out their stalks and white pith. Scrape out the seeds.

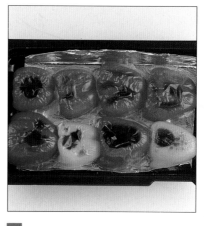

2 Line a broiler pan with foil and arrange the halved peppers, skin-side up in a single layer. Broil until the skins have blackened and blistered.

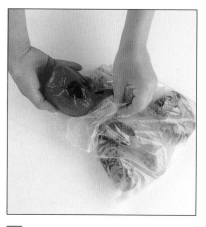

3 Transfer the peppers to a plastic bag and leave until cool, then peel away their skins and discard. Coarsely chop the pepper flesh.

4 Put the onion, garlic clove and ⅔ cup stock into a large saucepan. Boil for about 5 minutes until most of the stock has reduced in volume. Reduce the heat and stir until softened and beginning to color.

5 Sprinkle the flour over the onions, then gradually stir in the remaining stock. Add the chopped, roasted peppers and bring to a boil. Cover and simmer for a further 5 minutes.

6 Leave to cool slightly, then purée in a food processor or blender until smooth. Season to taste. Return to the saucepan and reheat until piping hot. Ladle into four soup bowls and garnish each with a sprinkling of diced peppers.

COOK'S TIP

If preferred, garnish the soup with a swirl of plain yogurt instead of the diced peppers.

Italian Vegetable Soup

The success of this clear soup depends on the quality of the stock, so use homemade vegetable stock rather than bouillon cubes.

Serves 4

INGREDIENTS
1 small carrot
1 baby leek
1 celery stalk
2 oz green cabbage
3¾ cups vegetable
    stock
1 bay leaf
1 cup cooked cannellini beans, rinsed
    and drained
⅕ cup soup pasta, such as tiny shells,
    bows, stars or elbows
salt and freshly ground black pepper
snipped fresh chives, to garnish

stock

cabbage

bay leaf

chives

baby leek

celery

carrot

pasta

1 Cut the carrot, leek and celery into 2 in long julienne strips. Slice the cabbage very finely.

2 Put the stock and bay leaf into a large saucepan and bring to a boil. Add the carrot, leek and celery, cover and simmer for 6 minutes.

NUTRITIONAL NOTES

PER SERVING:

CALORIES 69 **PROTEIN** 3.67 g
FAT 0.71 g **SATURATED FAT** 0.05 g
CARBOHYDRATE 12.68 g **FIBER** 2.82 g
ADDED SUGAR 0.05 g **SODIUM** 0.04 g

3 Add the cabbage, beans and pasta shapes. Stir, then simmer uncovered for a further 4-5 minutes, or until the vegetables and pasta are tender.

4 Remove the bay leaf and season to taste. Ladle into four soup bowls and garnish with snipped chives. Serve immediately.

Minted Melon and Grapefruit Cocktail

Melon is always a popular starter. Here the flavor is complemented by the refreshing taste of citrus fruit and a simple dressing.

Serves 4

INGREDIENTS
1 small cantaloupe, weighing about
 2¼ lb
2 pink grapefruits
1 yellow grapefruit
1 tsp Dijon mustard
1 tsp raspberry or sherry vinegar
1 tsp honey
1 tbsp chopped fresh mint
sprigs of fresh mint, to garnish

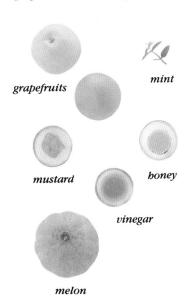

grapefruits

mint

mustard

honey

vinegar

melon

NUTRITIONAL NOTES
PER SERVING:

CALORIES 97 **PROTEIN** 2.22 g
FAT 0.63 g **SATURATED FAT** 0.00 g
CARBOHYDRATE 22.45 g **FIBER** 3.05 g
ADDED SUGAR 0.96 g **SODIUM** 0.24 g

1 Halve the melon and remove the seeds with a teaspoon. With a melon baller, carefully scoop the flesh into balls.

2 With a sharp knife, peel the grapefruit and remove all the white pith. Remove the segments by cutting between the membranes, holding the fruit over a small bowl to catch any juices.

3 Whisk the mustard, vinegar, honey, chopped mint and grapefruit juices together in a mixing bowl. Add the melon balls together with the grapefruit and mix well. Chill for 30 minutes.

4 Ladle into four dishes and serve garnished with a sprig of fresh mint.

Creamy Cod Chowder

Serve this soup as a substantial starter or snack, or as a light main meal accompanied by warm crusty whole wheat bread.

Serves 4–6

INGREDIENTS

12 oz smoked cod fillet
1 small onion, finely chopped
1 bay leaf
4 black peppercorns
3¾ cups skim milk
2 tsp cornstarch
7 oz canned corn kernels
1 tbsp chopped fresh parsley

NUTRITIONAL NOTES

PER SERVING:

CALORIES 200 **PROTEIN** 24.71 g
FAT 1.23 g **SATURATED FAT** 0.32 g
CARBOHYDRATE 23.88 g **FIBER** 0.85 g
ADDED SUGAR 2.44 g **SODIUM** 3.14 g

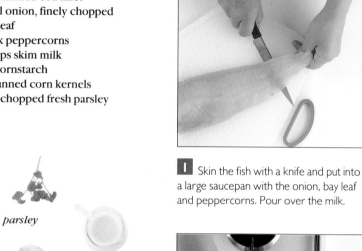

parsley

milk

cornstarch

bay leaf

onion

corn

cod fillet

1 Skin the fish with a knife and put into a large saucepan with the onion, bay leaf and peppercorns. Pour over the milk.

2 Bring to a boil. Reduce the heat and simmer very gently for 12-15 minutes, or until the fish is just cooked. Do not overcook.

3 Using a slotted spoon, lift out the fish and flake into large chunks. Remove the bay leaf and peppercorns and discard.

4 Blend the cornstarch with 2 tsp cold water and add to the saucepan. Bring to a boil and simmer for 1 minute or until slightly thickened.

5 Drain the corn kernels and add to the saucepan together with the flaked fish and parsley.

COOK'S TIP

The flavor of the chowder improves if made a day in advance. Chill in the refrigerator until required, then re-heat gently to prevent the fish from disintegrating.

6 Reheat the soup until piping hot, but do not boil. Ladle into four or six soup bowls and serve immediately.

Onions in Toast Cups

Fill crisp bread cups with tender pearl onions tossed in a mustardy glaze.

Serves 4–6

INGREDIENTS
12 thin slices of white bread
8 oz pearl onions or
   shallots
⅔ cup vegetable stock
1 tbsp dry white wine or dry
   sherry
2 turkey bacon rashers, cut into
   thin strips
2 tsp Worcestershire sauce
1 tsp tomato paste
¼ tsp prepared English mustard
salt and freshly ground black pepper
sprigs of Italian parsley, to garnish

pearl onions

stock

white bread

parsley

turkey rashers

NUTRITIONAL NOTES

PER SERVING:

CALORIES 178 **PROTEIN** 9.42 g
FAT 1.57 g **SATURATED FAT** 0.30 g
CARBOHYDRATE 33.26 g **FIBER** 1.82 g
ADDED SUGAR 0 **SODIUM** 1.23 g

1 Preheat the oven to 400°F. Stamp out the bread into rounds with a 3 in fluted cookie cutter and use to line a twelve-cup cupcake pan.

2 Cover each bread case with non-stick baking paper, and fill with baking beans or rice. Bake blind for 5 minutes in the preheated oven. Remove the paper and beans and continue to bake for a further 5 minutes, until lightly browned and crisp.

3 Meanwhile, put the pearl onions in a bowl and cover with boiling water. Leave for 3 minutes, then drain and rinse under cold water. Trim off their top and root ends and slip them out of their skins.

4 Simmer the onions and stock in a covered saucepan for 5 minutes. Uncover and cook, stirring occasionally until the stock has reduced entirely. Add all the remaining ingredients, except the parsley. Cook for 2-3 minutes. Fill the toast cups with the deviled onions. Serve hot, garnished with sprigs of Italian parsley.

Guacamole with Crudités

This fresh-tasting spicy dip is made using peas instead of the traditional avocados.

Serves 4–6

INGREDIENTS
2¼ cups frozen peas,
  defrosted
1 garlic clove, crushed
2 scallions, trimmed and
  chopped
1 tsp finely grated rind and juice
  of 1 lime
½ tsp ground cumin
dash of Tabasco sauce
1 tbsp reduced calorie
  mayonnaise
2 tbsp chopped fresh cilantro
salt and freshly ground black pepper
pinch of paprika and lime slices,
  to garnish

FOR THE CRUDITÉS
6 baby carrots
2 celery stalks
1 red-skinned apple
1 pear
1 tbsp lemon or lime juice
6 baby corn

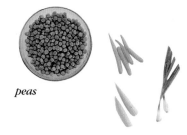

peas

vegetables

NUTRITIONAL NOTES

PER SERVING:

CALORIES 110 **PROTEIN** 6.22 g
FAT 2.29 g **SATURATED FAT** 0.49 g
CARBOHYDRATE 16.99 g **FIBER** 6.73 g
ADDED SUGAR 0.21 g **SODIUM** 0.19 g

1 Put the peas, garlic clove, scallions, lime rind and juice, cumin, Tabasco sauce, mayonnaise and salt and freshly ground black pepper into a food processor or a blender for a few minutes and process until smooth.

2 Add the chopped cilantro and process for a few more seconds. Spoon into a serving bowl, cover with plastic wrap and chill in the refrigerator for 30 minutes, to let the flavors develop.

3 For the crudités, trim and peel the carrots. Halve the celery stalks lengthwise and trim into sticks, the same length as the carrots. Quarter, core and thickly slice the apple and pear, then dip into the lemon or lime juice. Arrange with the baby corn on a platter.

4 Sprinkle the paprika over the guacamole and garnish with lime slices. Serve with the crudités.

Crunchy Baked Mushrooms with Dill Dip

These crispy-coated bites are ideal as an informal starter or served with drinks.

Serves 4–6

INGREDIENTS
2 cups fresh fine white bread
   crumbs
1½ tbsp finely grated sharp Cheddar
   cheese
1 tsp paprika
8 oz button mushrooms
2 egg whites

FOR THE TOMATO AND DILL DIP
4 ripe tomatoes
½ cup cottage cheese
4 tbsp natural low fat yogurt
1 garlic clove, crushed
2 tbsp chopped fresh dill
salt and freshly ground black pepper
sprig of fresh dill, to garnish

NUTRITIONAL NOTES
PER SERVING:

CALORIES 173 PROTEIN 11.88 g
FAT 6.04 g SATURATED FAT 3.24 g
CARBOHYDRATE 19.23 g FIBER 1.99 g
ADDED SUGAR 0 SODIUM 0.91 g

paprika

mushrooms

dill

tomatoes

bread crumbs

cottage cheese

1 Preheat the oven to 375°F. Mix together the bread crumbs, cheese and paprika in a bowl.

2 Wipe the mushrooms clean and trim the stems, if necessary. Lightly whisk the egg whites with a fork, until frothy.

3 Dip each mushroom into the egg whites, then into the bread crumb mixture. Repeat until all the mushrooms are coated.

4 Put the mushrooms on a non-stick baking sheet. Bake in the preheated oven for 15 minutes, or until tender and the coating has turned golden and crunchy.

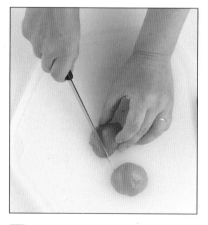

5 Meanwhile, to make the dip, plunge the tomatoes into a saucepan of boiling water for 1 minute, then into a saucepan of cold water. Slip off the skins. Halve, remove the seeds and cores and roughly chop the flesh.

6 Put the cottage cheese, yogurt, garlic clove and dill into a mixing bowl and combine well. Season to taste. Stir in the chopped tomatoes. Spoon the mixture into a serving dish and garnish with a sprig of fresh dill. Serve the mushrooms hot, together with the dip.

Herbed Fish Cakes with Lemon and Chive Sauce

The wonderful flavor of fresh herbs makes these fish cakes the catch of the day.

Serves 4

INGREDIENTS
12 oz potatoes, peeled
5 tbsp skimmed milk
12 oz haddock or flounder fillets,
  skinned
1 tbsp lemon juice
1 tbsp creamed horseradish
2 tbsp chopped fresh Italian
  parsley
flour, for dusting
2 cups fresh whole wheat
  bread crumbs
salt and freshly ground black pepper
sprig of Italian parsley, to garnish
snow peas and a sliced tomato and
  onion salad, to serve

FOR THE LEMON AND CHIVE SAUCE
thinly pared rind and juice of
  ½ small lemon
½ cup dry white wine
2 thin slices fresh ginger root
2 tsp cornstarch
2 tbsp snipped fresh chives

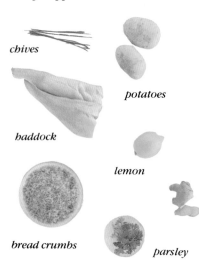

chives

potatoes

haddock

lemon

bread crumbs

ginger

parsley

1 Cook the potatoes in a large saucepan of boiling water for 15-20 minutes. Drain and mash with the milk and season to taste.

2 Purée the fish together with the lemon juice and horseradish in a blender or food processor. Mix together with the potatoes and parsley.

3 With floured hands, shape the mixture into eight fish cakes and coat with the bread crumbs. Chill in the refrigerator for 30 minutes.

4 Cook the fish cakes under a pre-heated moderate broiler for 5 minutes on each side, until browned.

5 To make the sauce, cut the lemon rind into julienne strips and put into a large saucepan together with the lemon juice, wine and ginger and season to taste.

NUTRITIONAL NOTES

PER SERVING:

CALORIES 232 **PROTEIN** 19.99 g
FAT 1.99 g **SATURATED FAT** 0.26 g
CARBOHYDRATE 30.62 g **FIBER** 3.11 g
ADDED SUGAR 0 **SODIUM** 0.82 g

6 Simmer uncovered for 6 minutes. Blend the cornstarch with 1 tbsp of cold water. Add to the saucepan and simmer until clear. Stir in the chives immediately before serving. Serve the sauce hot with the fish cakes, garnished with sprigs of Italian parsley and accompanied with snow peas and a sliced tomato and onion salad.

Cajun-style Cod

This recipe works equally well with any firm-fleshed fish such as swordfish, shark, tuna or halibut.

Serves 4

INGREDIENTS
4 cod steaks, each weighing
    about 6 oz
2 tbsp plain low fat yogurt
1 tbsp lime or lemon juice
1 garlic clove, crushed
1 tsp ground cumin
1 tsp paprika
1 tsp mustard powder
½ tsp cayenne pepper
½ tsp dried thyme
½ tsp dried oregano
baby potatoes and a mixed salad,
    to serve

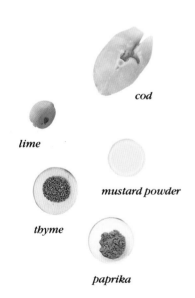

cod

lime

mustard powder

thyme

paprika

NUTRITIONAL NOTES

Per serving:

CALORIES 137 **PROTEIN** 28.42 g
FAT 1.75 g **SATURATED FAT** 0.26 g
CARBOHYDRATE 1.98 g **FIBER** 0.06 g
ADDED SUGAR 0 **SODIUM** 0.32 g

1 Pat the fish dry on absorbent paper towels. Mix together the yogurt and lime or lemon juice and brush lightly over both sides of the fish.

2 Mix together the garlic clove, spices and herbs. Coat both sides of the fish with the seasoning mix, rubbing in well.

COOK'S TIP

If you don't have a ridged broiler pan, heat several metal skewers under a broiler until red hot. Holding the ends with a cloth, press onto the seasoned fish before cooking to give a seared appearance.

3 Spray a ridged broiler pan or heavy-based frying pan with non-stick cooking spray. Heat until very hot. Add the fish and cook over a high heat for 4 minutes, or until the underside is well browned.

4 Turn over and cook for a further 4 minutes, or until the steaks have cooked through. Serve immediately accompanied with baby potatoes and a mixed salad.

Sand Dab Provençal

Recreate the taste of the Mediterranean with this easy-to-make fish casserole.

Serves 4

INGREDIENTS

4 large sand dab fillets
2 small red onions
½ cup vegetable stock
4 tbsp dry red wine
1 garlic clove, crushed
2 zucchini, sliced
1 yellow bell pepper, seeded and
    sliced
14 oz can chopped tomatoes
1 tbsp chopped fresh thyme
salt and freshly ground black pepper
Potato Gratin, to serve

chopped tomatoes

plaice

thyme

zucchini

red onion   *bell pepper*

NUTRITIONAL NOTES

PER SERVING:

CALORIES 191 **PROTEIN** 29.46 g
FAT 3.77 g **SATURATED FAT** 0.61 g
CARBOHYDRATE 8.00 g **FIBER** 1.97 g
ADDED SUGAR 0 **SODIUM** 0.57 g

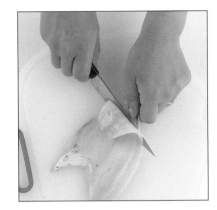

1 Preheat the oven to 350°F. Skin the sand dab fillets with a sharp knife by laying them skin-side down. Holding the tail end, push the knife between the skin and flesh in a sawing movement. Hold the knife at an angle with the blade towards the skin.

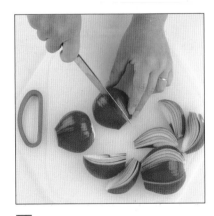

2 Cut each onion into eight wedges. Put into a heavy-based saucepan with the stock. Cover and simmer for 5 minutes. Uncover and continue to cook, stirring occasionally, until the stock has reduced entirely. Add the wine and garlic clove to the pan and continue to cook until the onions are soft.

3 Add the zucchini, yellow pepper, tomatoes and thyme and season to taste. Simmer for 3 minutes. Spoon the sauce into a large casserole.

4 Fold each fillet in half and place on top of the sauce. Cover and cook in the preheated oven for 15-20 minutes until the fish is opaque and cooked. Serve with Potato Gratin.

Seafood Pasta Shells with Spinach Sauce

You'll need very large pasta shells, measuring about 1½ in long for this dish; don't try stuffing smaller shells – it's much too fussy!

Serves 4

INGREDIENTS

1 tbsp low fat spread
8 scallions, finely sliced
6 tomatoes
32 large dried pasta shells
1 cup low fat cream cheese
6 tbsp skim milk
pinch of freshly grated nutmeg
8 oz shrimp
6 oz can white crabmeat, drained and flaked
4 oz frozen chopped spinach, thawed and drained
salt and freshly ground black pepper

scallions

shrimp

pasta shells

crabmeat

spinach

tomatoes

NUTRITIONAL NOTES
PER SERVING:

CALORIES 399 PROTEIN 32.69 g
FAT 12.79 g SATURATED FAT 5.81 g
CARBOHYDRATE 40.75 g FIBER 3.31 g
ADDED SUGAR 0 SODIUM 3.59 g

1 Preheat the oven to 300°F. Melt the low fat spread in a small saucepan and gently cook the scallions for 3-4 minutes, or until softened.

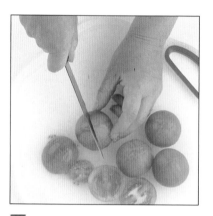

2 Plunge the tomatoes into a saucepan of boiling water for 1 minute, then into a saucepan of cold water. Slip off the skins. Halve the tomatoes, remove the seeds and cores and roughly chop the flesh.

3 Cook the pasta shells in lightly salted boiling water for about 10 minutes, or until *al dente*. Drain well.

4 Put the low fat cream cheese and skim milk into a saucepan and heat gently, stirring until blended. Season with salt, freshly ground black pepper and a pinch of nutmeg. Measure 2 tbsp of the sauce into a bowl.

5 Add the scallions, tomatoes, shrimp, and crabmeat to the bowl. Mix well. Spoon the filling into the shells and place in a single layer in a shallow ovenproof dish. Cover with foil and cook in the preheated oven for 10 minutes.

6 Stir the spinach into the remaining sauce. Bring to a boil and simmer gently for 1 minute, stirring all the time. Drizzle over the pasta shells and serve hot.

Marinated Monkfish and Mussel Skewers

You can cook these fish kebabs on the barbecue – when the weather allows!

Serves 4

INGREDIENTS
1 lb monkfish, skinned and
   boned
1 tsp olive oil
2 tbsp lemon juice
1 tsp paprika
1 garlic clove, crushed
4 turkey bacon rashers
8 cooked mussels
8 raw shrimp
1 tbsp chopped fresh dill
salt and freshly ground black pepper
lemon wedges, to garnish
salad leaves and long-grain and wild
   rice, to serve

mussels

turkey rashers

dill

lemon

monkfish

NUTRITIONAL NOTES

PER SERVING:

CALORIES 133 **PROTEIN** 25.46 g
FAT 3.23 g **SATURATED FAT** 0.77 g
CARBOHYDRATE 0.61 g **FIBER** 0.12 g
ADDED SUGAR 0 **SODIUM** 0.43 g

1 Cut the monkfish into 1 in cubes and place in a shallow glass dish. Mix together the oil, lemon juice, paprika, and garlic clove and season with pepper.

2 Pour the marinade over the fish and toss to coat evenly. Cover and leave in a cool place for 30 minutes.

COOK'S TIP

Monkfish is ideal for kebabs, but can be expensive. Cod makes a good alternative.

3 Cut the turkey rashers in half and wrap each strip around a mussel. Thread onto skewers alternating with the fish cubes and raw shrimp.

4 Cook the kebabs under a hot broiler for 7-8 minutes, turning once and basting with the marinade. Sprinkle with chopped dill and salt. Garnish with lemon wedges and serve with salad and rice.

Lemon Sole baked in a Paper Case

Make sure that these paper parcels are well sealed, so that none of the delicious juices can escape.

Serves 4

INGREDIENTS
4 lemon sole fillets, each weighing
    about 5 oz
½ small cucumber, sliced
4 lemon slices
4 tbsp dry white wine
sprigs of fresh dill, to garnish
new potatoes and braised celery,
    to serve

FOR THE YOGURT HOLLANDAISE
¼ pint plain low fat yogurt
1 tsp lemon juice
2 egg yolks
1 tsp Dijon mustard
salt and freshly ground black pepper

sole

dill

cucumber

egg

lemon

mustard

NUTRITIONAL NOTES
PER SERVING:

CALORIES 185 **PROTEIN** 29.27 g
FAT 4.99 g **SATURATED FAT** 1.58 g
CARBOHYDRATE 3.72 g **FIBER** 0.27 g
ADDED SUGAR 0 **SODIUM** 0.55 g

1 Preheat the oven to 350°F. Cut out four heart shapes from non-stick baking paper, each about 8 × 6 in.

2 Place a sole fillet on one side of each heart. Arrange the cucumber and lemon slices on top of each fillet. Sprinkle with the wine and close the parcels by turning the edges of the paper and twisting to secure. Put on a baking tray and cook in the preheated oven for 15 minutes.

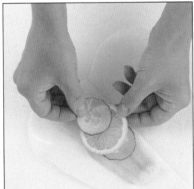

3 For the hollandaise, beat together the yogurt, lemon juice and egg yolks in a double boiler or bowl placed over a saucepan. Cook over simmering water, stirring for 15 minutes, or until thickened. (The sauce will become thinner after 10 minutes, but will thicken again.)

4 Remove from the heat and stir in the mustard. Season to taste with salt and freshly ground black pepper. Open the fish parcels, garnish with a sprig of dill and serve accompanied with the sauce, new potatoes and braised celery.

Smoked Trout Cannelloni

Smoked trout can be bought already filleted or whole.
If you buy fillets, you'll need 8 oz of fish.

Serves 4–6

INGREDIENTS
1 large onion, finely chopped
1 garlic clove, crushed
4 tbsp vegetable stock
2 × 14 oz cans chopped tomatoes
½ tsp dried mixed herbs
1 smoked trout, weighing about
    14 oz
¾ cup frozen peas, thawed
1½ cups fresh bread crumbs
16 cannelloni tubes, cooked
salt and freshly ground black pepper
mixed salad, to serve

FOR THE CHEESE SAUCE
2 tbsp low fat spread
¼ cup flour
1½ cups skim milk
freshly grated nutmeg
1½ tbsp freshly grated Parmesan
    cheese

mixed herbs

trout

onion

tomato

chopped tomatoes

cannelloni

1 Simmer the onion, garlic clove and stock in a large covered saucepan for 3 minutes. Uncover and continue to cook, stirring occasionally, until the stock has reduced entirely.

2 Stir in the tomatoes and dried herbs. Simmer uncovered for a further 10 minutes, or until very thick.

3 Meanwhile, skin the smoked trout with a sharp knife. Carefully flake the flesh and discard all the bones. Mix the fish together with the tomato mixture, peas, bread crumbs, salt and freshly ground black pepper.

4 Preheat the oven to 375°F. Spoon the filling into the cannelloni tubes and arrange in an ovenproof dish.

5 For the sauce, put the low fat spread, flour and milk into a saucepan and cook over a medium heat, whisking constantly until the sauce thickens. Simmer for 2-3 minutes, stirring all the time. Season to taste with salt, freshly ground black pepper and nutmeg.

NUTRITIONAL NOTES

PER SERVING:

CALORIES 441 **PROTEIN** 31.36 g
FAT 8.57 g **SATURATED FAT** 2.41 g
CARBOHYDRATE 63.83 g **FIBER** 4.94 g
ADDED SUGAR 0 **SODIUM** 0.95 g

COOK'S TIP

You can use a 7 oz can of tuna in
water in place of the trout, if
preferred.

6 Pour the sauce over the cannelloni
and sprinkle with the grated Parmesan
cheese. Bake in the preheated oven for
35-40 minutes, or until the top is golden
and bubbling. Serve with a mixed salad.

Turkey and Tomato Ragu

Turkey is not just for festive occasions. Here, it's turned into tasty meatballs and simmered with rice in a tomato sauce.

Serves 4

INGREDIENTS
1 oz white bread, crusts removed
2 tbsp skim milk
1 garlic clove, crushed
½ tsp caraway seeds
8 oz ground turkey
1 egg white
1½ cups fresh or canned low salt
   chicken stock
14 oz can plum tomatoes
1 tbsp tomato paste
½ cup rice
salt and freshly ground black pepper
1 tbsp chopped fresh basil, to garnish
carrot and zucchini ribbons, to serve

basil

ground turkey

rice

bread

tomato paste

plum tomatoes

caraway seeds

garlic

COOK'S TIP
To make carrot and zucchini ribbons, cut the vegetables lengthwise into thin strips using a vegetable peeler, and blanch or steam until cooked through.

NUTRITIONAL NOTES

PER SERVING:

CALORIES 190 PROTEIN 18.04 g
FAT 1.88 g SATURATED FAT 0.24 g
CARBOHYDRATE 26.96 g FIBER 1.04 g
ADDED SUGAR 0 SODIUM 0.32 g

1 Cut the bread into small cubes and put into a mixing bowl. Sprinkle over the milk and leave to soak for 5 minutes.

2 Add the garlic clove, caraway seeds, turkey, salt and freshly ground black pepper to the bread. Mix together well.

3 Whisk the egg white until stiff, then fold, half at a time, into the turkey mixture. Chill for 10 minutes in the refrigerator.

4 Put the stock, tomatoes and tomato paste into a large, heavy-based saucepan and bring to a boil.

5 Add the rice, stir and cook briskly for about 5 minutes. Turn the heat down to a gentle simmer.

6 Meanwhile, shape the turkey mixture into 16 small balls. Carefully drop them into the tomato stock and simmer for a further 8-10 minutes, or until the turkey balls and rice are cooked. Garnish with chopped basil, and serve with carrot and zucchini ribbons.

Turkey Tonnato

This low fat version of the Italian dish 'vitello tonnato' is garnished with fine strips of red pepper instead of the traditional anchovy fillets.

NUTRITIONAL NOTES

PER SERVING:

CALORIES 235 **PROTEIN** 35.47 g
FAT 7.09 g **SATURATED FAT** 1.33 g
CARBOHYDRATE 7.80 g **FIBER** 1.37 g
ADDED SUGAR 1.04 g **SODIUM** 0.87 g

Serves 4

INGREDIENTS
1 lb turkey fillets
1 small onion, sliced
1 bay leaf
4 black peppercorns
1½ cups fresh chicken stock
7 oz can tuna in water, drained
5 tbsp reduced calorie mayonnaise
2 tbsp lemon juice
2 red bell peppers, seeded and
    thinly sliced
about 25 capers, drained
pinch of salt
mixed salad and tomatoes, to serve

tuna

lemon

onion

bay leaf

capers

mayonnaise

pepper

turkey fillet

stock

1 Put the turkey fillets in a single layer in a large, heavy-based saucepan. Add the onion, bay leaf, peppercorns and stock. Bring to a boil and reduce the heat. Cover and simmer for 12 minutes, or until tender.

2 Turn off the heat and leave the turkey to cool in the stock, then remove with a slotted spoon. Slice thickly and arrange on a serving plate.

3 Boil the stock until reduced to about 5 tbsp. Strain and leave to cool.

4 Put the tuna, mayonnaise, lemon juice, 3 tbsp of the reduced stock and salt into a blender or food processor and purée until smooth.

5 Stir in enough of the remaining stock to reduce the sauce to the thickness of heavy cream. Spoon over the turkey.

6 Arrange the strips of red pepper in a lattice pattern over the turkey. Put a caper in the center of each square. Chill in the refrigerator for 1 hour and serve with a fresh mixed salad and tomatoes.

Fragrant Chicken Curry

In this dish, the spiced sauce is thickened using lentils rather than the traditional onions fried in butter.

Serves 4

INGREDIENTS
½ cup red lentils
2 tbsp mild curry powder
2 tsp ground coriander
1 tsp cumin seeds
2 cups vegetable stock
8 chicken thighs, skinned
8 oz fresh shredded, or frozen
  spinach, thawed and well drained
1 tbsp chopped fresh coriander
salt and freshly ground black pepper
sprigs of fresh cilantro, to garnish
white or brown basmati rice and
  broiled papadums, to serve

cilantro

spinach

cumin seeds

curry powder

ground cilantro

lentils

chicken thigh

1 Rinse the lentils under cold running water. Put into a large, heavy-based saucepan with the curry powder, ground coriander, cumin seeds and stock.

2 Bring to a boil then lower the heat. Cover and gently simmer for 10 minutes.

NUTRITIONAL NOTES
PER SERVING:

CALORIES 228 **PROTEIN** 26.51 g
FAT 7.43 g **SATURATED FAT** 1.91 g
CARBOHYDRATE 14.76 g **FIBER** 3.83 g
ADDED SUGAR 0 **SODIUM** 0.54 g

3 Add the chicken and spinach. Re-cover and simmer gently for a further 40 minutes, or until the chicken has cooked.

4 Stir in the chopped cilantro and season to taste. Serve garnished with fresh cilantro and accompanied by the rice and broiled papadums.

Chicken with Orange and Mustard Sauce

The beauty of this recipe is its simplicity; the chicken continues to cook in its own juices while you prepare the sauce.

Serves 4

INGREDIENTS
2 large oranges
4 chicken breasts, boned and skinned
1 tsp sunflower oil
salt and freshly ground black pepper
baby potatoes and sliced zucchini
tossed in parsley, to serve

FOR THE ORANGE AND MUSTARD SAUCE
2 tsp cornstarch
⅔ cup strained yogurt
1 tsp Dijon mustard

chicken breast

yogurt

cornstarch

mustard

orange

NUTRITIONAL NOTES

PER SERVING:

CALORIES 251 **PROTEIN** 35.87 g
FAT 6.07 g **SATURATED FAT** 1.88 g
CARBOHYDRATE 14.16 g **FIBER** 1.79 g
ADDED SUGAR 0 **SODIUM** 0.46 g

1 Peel the oranges using a sharp knife, removing all the white pith. Remove the segments by cutting between the membranes, holding the fruit over a small bowl to catch any juice. Set aside with the juice until required.

2 Season the chicken with salt and freshly ground black pepper. Heat the oil in a non-stick frying pan and cook the chicken for 5 minutes on each side. Take out of the frying pan and wrap in foil; the meat will continue to cook for a while.

3 For the sauce, blend together the cornstarch with the juice from the orange. Add the yogurt and mustard. Put into the frying pan and slowly bring to a boil. Simmer for 1 minute.

4 Add the orange segments to the sauce and heat gently. Unwrap the chicken and add any excess juices to the sauce. Slice on the diagonal and serve with the sauce, baby potatoes and sliced zucchini tossed in parsley.

Chicken Kiev

Cut through the crispy-coated chicken to reveal a creamy filling with just a hint of garlic.

Serves 4

INGREDIENTS
4 large chicken breasts, boned and
    skinned
1 tbsp lemon juice
½ cup ricotta cheese
1 garlic clove, crushed
2 tbsp chopped fresh parsley
¼ tsp freshly grated nutmeg
2 tbsp flour
pinch of cayenne pepper
¼ tsp salt
2 cups fresh white bread
    crumbs
2 egg whites, lightly beaten
duchesse potatoes, green beans and
    broiled tomatoes, to serve

bread crumbs

egg whites

chicken breast

ricotta cheese

garlic

parsley

1 Preheat the oven to 400°F. Place the chicken breasts between two sheets of plastic wrap and gently beat with a rolling pin until flattened. Sprinkle with the lemon juice.

2 Mix the ricotta cheese with the garlic, 1 tbsp of the chopped parsley, and the nutmeg. Shape into four 2-in long cylinders.

3 Put one portion of the cheese and herb mixture in the center of each chicken breast and fold the meat over, tucking in the edges to enclose the filling completely.

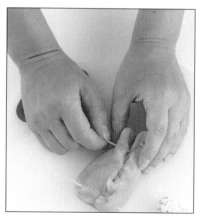

4 Secure the chicken with toothpicks pushed through the center of each. Mix together the flour, cayenne pepper and salt. Dust the chicken with the flour.

5 Mix together the bread crumbs and remaining parsley. Dip the chicken into the egg whites, then coat with the bread crumbs. Chill for 30 minutes in the refrigerator, then dip into the egg white and bread crumbs for a second time.

NUTRITIONAL NOTES

PER SERVING:

CALORIES 320 **PROTEIN** 40.27 g
FAT 8.81 g **SATURATED FAT** 1.72 g
CARBOHYDRATE 21.17 g **FIBER** 0.97 g
ADDED SUGAR 0 **SODIUM** 1.11 g

6 Put the chicken on a non-stick baking sheet and spray with non-stick cooking spray. Bake in the preheated oven for 25 minutes or until the coating is golden brown and the chicken completely cooked. Remove the toothpicks and serve with duchesse potatoes, green beans and broiled tomatoes.

Hot and Sour Pork

Chinese five-spice powder is made from a mixture of ground star anise, Szechuan pepper, cassia, cloves and fennel seed and has a flavor similar to liquorice. If you can't find any, use mixed spice instead.

NUTRITIONAL NOTES

Per serving:

CALORIES 196 PROTEIN 19.78 g
FAT 7.29 g SATURATED FAT 2.37 g
CARBOHYDRATE 13.63 g FIBER 1.16 g
ADDED SUGAR 0 SODIUM 0.77 g

Serves 4

INGREDIENTS
12 oz pork fillet
1 tsp sunflower oil
1 in piece ginger root, grated
1 red chili, seeded and finely chopped
1 tsp Chinese five-spice powder
1 tbsp sherry vinegar
1 tbsp soy sauce
8 oz can pineapple chunks in natural juice
¾ cup chicken stock
4 tsp cornstarch
1 small green bell pepper, seeded and sliced
4 oz baby corn, halved
salt and freshly ground black pepper
sprig of Italian parsley, to garnish
boiled rice, to serve

pineapple chunks

pork fillet

chili

cornstarch

soy sauce

bell pepper

baby corn

1 Preheat the oven to 325°F. Trim away any visible fat from the pork and cut into ½ in thick slices.

2 Brush the sunflower oil over the base of a flameproof casserole. Heat over a medium flame, then fry the meat for about 2 minutes on each side or until lightly browned.

3 Blend together the ginger, chili, five-spice powder, vinegar and soy sauce.

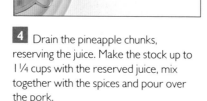

4 Drain the pineapple chunks, reserving the juice. Make the stock up to 1¼ cups with the reserved juice, mix together with the spices and pour over the pork.

5 Slowly bring to a boil. Blend the cornstarch with 1 tbsp of cold water and gradually stir into the pork. Add the vegetables and season to taste.

6 Cover and cook in the oven for 30 minutes. Stir in the pineapple and cook for a further 5 minutes. Garnish with Italian parsley and serve with boiled rice.

Honey-roast Pork with Thyme and Rosemary

Herbs and honey add flavor and sweetness to tenderloin – the leanest cut of pork.

NUTRITIONAL NOTES

PER SERVING:

CALORIES 256 PROTEIN 25.01 g
FAT 8.92 g SATURATED FAT 2.92 g
CARBOHYDRATE 18.09 g FIBER 1.10 g
ADDED SUGAR 10.57 g SODIUM 0.79 g

Serves 4

INGREDIENTS
1 lb pork tenderloin
2 tbsp honey
2 tbsp Dijon mustard
1 tsp chopped fresh rosemary
½ tsp chopped fresh thyme
¼ tsp whole pink and green
    peppercorns
sprigs of fresh rosemary and thyme, to
    garnish
Potato Gratin and cauliflower,
    to serve

FOR THE RED ONION CONFIT
4 red onions
1½ cups vegetable stock
1 tbsp red wine vinegar
1 tbsp superfine sugar
1 garlic clove, crushed
2 tbsp ruby port
pinch of salt

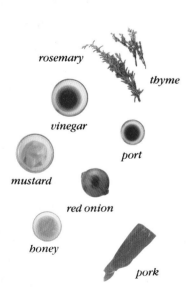

rosemary
thyme
vinegar
port
mustard
red onion
honey
pork

1 Preheat the oven to 350°F. Trim off any visible fat from the pork. Put the honey, mustard, rosemary and thyme in a small bowl and mix them together well.

2 Crush the peppercorns using a pestle and mortar. Spread the honey mixture over the pork and sprinkle with the crushed peppercorns. Place in a non-stick roasting pan and cook in the preheated oven for 35-45 minutes.

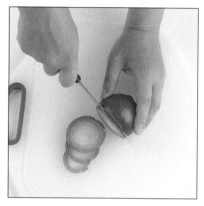

3 For the red onion confit, slice the onions into rings and put them into a heavy-based saucepan.

4 Add the stock, vinegar, sugar and garlic clove to the saucepan. Bring to a boil, then reduce the heat. Cover and simmer for 15 minutes.

5 Uncover and pour in the port and continue to simmer, stirring occasionally, until the onions are soft and the juices thick and syrupy. Season to taste with salt.

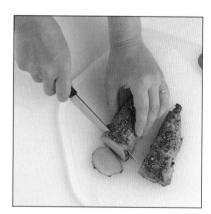

6 Cut the pork into slices and arrange on four warmed plates. Serve garnished with rosemary and thyme and accompanied with the red onion confit, Potato Gratin and cauliflower.

Lamb Tagine with Fruit

The slightly sharp taste of dried fruits complements
the richness of lamb in this satisfying casserole.

Serves 4

INGREDIENTS

12 oz mixed dried fruit such
  as apple rings, apricots, pears
  and prunes
1½ lb boned lean lamb
1 onion, sliced
½ tsp ground ginger
1 tsp ground cilantro
large pinch of saffron strands
1 cinnamon stick
juice of 1 lemon
3⅔ cups vegetable
  stock
1 tsp chopped fresh thyme
1 tbsp honey
¼ cup blanched almonds, split and
  toasted, to garnish
sprig of fresh thyme, to garnish
steamed couscous, to serve

dried fruit

thyme

almonds

lamb

NUTRITIONAL NOTES

PER SERVING:

CALORIES 580 **PROTEIN** 40.05 g
FAT 18.94 g **SATURATED FAT** 7.37 g
CARBOHYDRATE 66.69 g **FIBER** 2.81 g
ADDED SUGAR 2.87 g **SODIUM** 1.11 g

1 Rinse the dried fruit under cold
running water. Put it into a large bowl and
cover with plenty of cold water. Leave to
soak for 4 hours.

2 Trim away any visible fat from the
lamb and cut into 1 in cubes. Add it to a
large, heavy-based saucepan together
with the onion, spices, lemon juice and
stock. Bring to a boil, and cover with a
tight fitting lid. Simmer over a low heat
for 2 hours.

3 Leave to cool, then chill in the
refrigerator for at least 2 hours or until
the fat solidifies on the top. Skim off the
fat and discard.

4 Drain the fruit and add to the lamb
together with the thyme and honey.
Simmer uncovered for 15 minutes. Spoon
into a warmed serving dish and garnish
with toasted almonds and fresh thyme.
Serve with steamed couscous.

Stir-fried Beef and Broccoli

This spicy beef may be served with noodles or on a bed of boiled rice for a speedy and low calorie Chinese meal.

Serves 4

INGREDIENTS

12 oz sirloin or lean London
   broil steak
1 tbsp cornstarch
1 tsp sesame oil
12 oz broccoli, cut into small
   florets
4 scallions, sliced on the diagonal
1 carrot, cut into matchstick strips
1 garlic clove, crushed
1 in piece ginger root, cut into very
   fine strips
½ cup low fat beef stock
2 tbsp soy sauce
2 tbsp dry sherry
2 tsp light brown sugar
scallion tassels, to garnish
noodles or rice, to serve

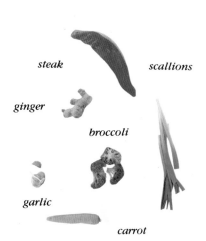

steak   *scallions*

ginger

broccoli

garlic

carrot

NUTRITIONAL NOTES

PER SERVING:

CALORIES 195 **PROTEIN** 22.84 g
FAT 6.21 g **SATURATED FAT** 1.81 g
CARBOHYDRATE 10.35 g **FIBER** 2.87 g
ADDED SUGAR 2.67 g **SODIUM** 1.36 g

1 Trim the beef and cut into thin slices across the grain. Cut each slice into thin strips. Toss in the cornstarch to coat thoroughly.

2 Heat the sesame oil in a large non-stick frying pan or wok. Add the beef strips and stir-fry over a brisk heat for 3 minutes. Remove and set aside.

COOK'S TIP

To make scallion tassels, trim the bulb base then cut the green shoot so that the onion is 3 in long. Shred to within 1 in of the base and put into iced water for 1 hour.

3 Add the broccoli, scallions, carrot, garlic clove, ginger and stock to the frying pan or wok. Cover and simmer for 3 minutes. Uncover and cook, stirring until all the stock has reduced entirely.

4 Mix the soy sauce, sherry and brown sugar together. Add to the frying pan or wok with the beef. Cook for 2–3 minutes stirring continuously. Spoon into a warm serving dish and garnish with scallion tassels. Serve on a bed of noodles or rice.

Burgundy Steak and Mushroom Pie

Tender chunks of beef are cooked in a rich wine sauce and a crisp filo pastry crust. It won't pile on the calories, although it may taste that way.

Serves 4

INGREDIENTS
1 onion, finely chopped
¾ cup low fat beef stock
1 lb lean sirloin or top round steak,
   cut into 1 in cubes
½ cup dry red wine
3 tbsp flour
8 oz button mushrooms, halved
5 sheets filo pastry
2 tsp sunflower oil
salt and freshly ground black pepper
mashed potatoes and wax beans,
   to serve

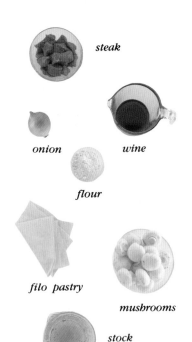

steak

onion   wine

flour

filo pastry

mushrooms

stock

1 Simmer the onion with ½ cup of the stock in a large covered non-stick saucepan for 5 minutes. Uncover and continue to cook, stirring occasionally, until the stock has reduced entirely. Transfer to a plate and set aside until required.

2 Add the steak to the saucepan and dry-fry until the meat is lightly browned. Return the onions to the saucepan together with the remaining stock and the red wine. Cover and simmer gently for about 1½ hours, or until tender.

3 Preheat the oven to 375°F. Blend the flour with 3 tbsp of cold water, add to the saucepan and simmer, stirring all the time until the sauce has thickened.

4 Add the mushrooms and continue to cook for 3 minutes. Season to taste and spoon into a 5 cup pie dish.

5 Brush a sheet of filo pastry with a little of the oil, then crumple it up loosely and place oil-side up over the filling. Repeat with the remaining pastry and oil.

NUTRITIONAL NOTES

PER SERVING:

CALORIES 282 **PROTEIN** 26.82 g
FAT 7.77 g **SATURATED FAT** 2.49 g
CARBOHYDRATE 22.49 g **FIBER** 1.39 g
ADDED SUGAR 0.46 g **SODIUM** 0.77 g

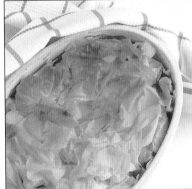

6 Bake in the oven for 25-30 minutes, until the pastry is golden brown and crispy. Serve with mashed potatoes and wax beans.

Vegetarian Cassoulet

Every town in southwest France has its own version of this popular classic. Warm French bread is all that is needed to complete this hearty vegetable version.

COOK'S TIP

COOK'S TIP

If you're short of time use canned navy beans – you'll need two 14 oz cans. Drain, reserving the bean juices and make up to 1⅔ cups with vegetable stock.

Serves 4–6

INGREDIENTS
2 cups dried navy beans
1 bay leaf
2 onions
3 whole cloves
2 garlic cloves, crushed
1 tsp olive oil
2 leeks, thickly sliced
12 baby carrots
4 oz button mushrooms
14 oz can chopped tomatoes
1 tbsp tomato paste
1 tsp paprika
1 tbsp chopped fresh thyme
2 tbsp chopped fresh parsley
2 cups fresh white bread crumbs
salt and freshly ground black pepper
sprig of fresh thyme, to garnish

1 Soak the beans overnight in plenty of cold water. Drain and rinse under cold running water. Put them in a saucepan together with 7½ cups of cold water and the bay leaf. Bring to a boil and cook rapidly for 10 minutes.

2 Peel one of the onions and spike with cloves. Add to the beans and reduce the heat. Cover and simmer gently for 1 hour, until the beans are almost tender. Drain, reserving the stock but discarding the bay leaf and onion.

3 Chop the remaining onion and put it into a large flameproof casserole together with the garlic cloves and olive oil. Cook gently for 5 minutes, or until softened.

chopped tomatoes   *bay leaf*

leek

bread crumbs

carrots   *mushrooms*

4 Preheat the oven to 325°F. Add the leeks, carrots, mushrooms, chopped tomatoes, tomato paste, paprika, thyme and 1⅔ cups of the reserved stock to the casserole.

5 Bring to a boil, cover and simmer gently for 10 minutes. Stir in the cooked beans and parsley. Season to taste.

NUTRITIONAL NOTES

Per serving:

CALORIES 434 **PROTEIN** 27.78 g
FAT 3.96 g **SATURATED FAT** 0.46 g
CARBOHYDRATE 76.64 g **FIBER** 21.57 g
ADDED SUGAR 0 **SODIUM** 0.66 g

6 Sprinkle with the bread crumbs and bake uncovered in the preheated oven for 35 minutes, or until the topping is golden brown and crisp. Serve garnished with a sprig of fresh thyme.

Pasta with Pesto Sauce

Traditionally made with a lot of olive oil, this simple pesto sauce is still full of flavor but relatively low in fat.

Serves 4

INGREDIENTS
2 cups dried pasta such as spirals or
  bows
1 cup fresh basil leaves
½ cup parsley sprigs
1 garlic clove, crushed
¼ cup pine nuts
½ cup cottage cheese
2 tbsp freshly grated Parmesan cheese
salt and freshly ground black pepper
few sprigs of fresh basil, to garnish

pine nuts   *pasta*

basil

cottage cheese

Parmesan

NUTRITIONAL NOTES
PER SERVING:

CALORIES 331 PROTEIN 15.54 g
FAT 11.30 g SATURATED FAT 4.33 g
CARBOHYDRATE 44.59 g FIBER 2.23 g
ADDED SUGAR 0 SODIUM 0.56 g

1 Cook the pasta in plenty of lightly salted rapidly boiling water in a large saucepan for 8-10 minutes or until *al dente*. Drain well.

2 Meanwhile put half the basil and half the parsley, the garlic clove, pine nuts and cottage cheese into a food processor or blender fitted with a metal blade and process until smooth.

3 Add the remaining basil and parsley together with the Parmesan cheese and seasoning. Process until the herbs are finely chopped.

4 Toss the pasta with the pesto and serve on warmed plates. Garnish with fresh basil sprigs.

Cheese and Onion Pie

This inexpensive supper dish is made substantial with the addition of rolled oats.

Serves 4

INGREDIENTS
2 large onions, thinly sliced
1 garlic clove, crushed
⅔ cup vegetable stock
3 cups rolled oats
1 cup grated Edam cheese
2 tbsp chopped fresh parsley
2 eggs, lightly beaten
1 medium potato, peeled
salt and freshly ground black pepper
coleslaw and tomatoes, halved,
    to serve

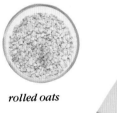

rolled oats

Edam cheese

eggs

parsley

onion

potato

NUTRITIONAL NOTES

PER SERVING:

CALORIES 436 **PROTEIN** 20.68 g
FAT 15.81 g **SATURATED FAT** 6.50 g
CARBOHYDRATE 56.38 g **FIBER** 6.18 g
ADDED SUGAR 0 **SODIUM** 1.05 g

1 Preheat the oven to 350°F. Line the base of a 8 in sandwich pie pan with non-stick baking paper. Put the onions, garlic clove and stock into a heavy-based saucepan and simmer until the stock has reduced entirely.

2 Spread the oats on a baking sheet and toast in the oven for 10 minutes. Mix with the onions, cheese, parsley, eggs, salt and freshly ground black pepper.

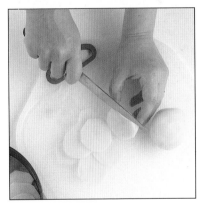

3 Thinly slice the potato and use it to line the base of the pan. Spoon in the oat mixture. Cover with a piece of foil.

4 Bake in the preheated oven for 35 minutes. Turn out onto a baking sheet and remove the lining paper. Put under a preheated hot broiler to brown the potatoes. Cut into wedges and serve hot with coleslaw and halved tomatoes.

Carrot Mousse with Mushroom Sauce

The combination of fresh vegetables in this impressive yet easy-to-make mousse make healthy eating a pleasure.

NUTRITIONAL NOTES

PER SERVING:

CALORIES 174 **PROTEIN** 12.65 g
FAT 5.90 g **SATURATED FAT** 1.44 g
CARBOHYDRATE 18.69 g **FIBER** 3.13 g
ADDED SUGAR 0 **SODIUM** 0.42 g

Serves 4

INGREDIENTS

12 oz carrots, roughly chopped
1 small red bell pepper, seeded and
   roughly chopped
3 tbsp vegetable stock or water
2 eggs
1 egg white
½ cup quark or low fat cream cheese
1 tbsp chopped fresh tarragon
salt and freshly ground black pepper
sprig of fresh tarragon, to garnish
boiled rice and leeks, to serve

FOR THE MUSHROOM SAUCE

2 tbsp low fat spread
6 oz mushrooms, sliced
2 tbsp flour
1 cup skim milk

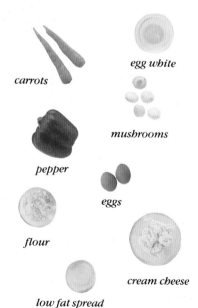

carrots

egg white

mushrooms

pepper

eggs

flour

cream cheese

low fat spread

1 Preheat the oven to 375°F. Line the bases of four ⅔ cup ramekin dishes with non-stick baking paper. Put the carrots and red pepper in a small saucepan with the vegetable stock or water. Cover and cook for 5 minutes, or until tender. Drain well.

2 Lightly beat the eggs and egg white together. Mix with the quark or low fat cream cheese. Season to taste. Purée the cooked vegetables in a food processor or blender. Add the cheese mixture and process for a few seconds more until smooth. Stir in the chopped tarragon.

3 Divide the carrot mixture between the prepared ramekin dishes and cover with foil. Place the dishes in a roasting pan half-filled with hot water. Bake in the oven for 35 minutes, or until set.

4 For the mushroom sauce, melt 1 tbsp of the low fat spread in a frying pan. Add the mushrooms and gently sauté for 5 minutes, until soft.

5 Put the remaining low fat spread in a small saucepan together with the flour and milk. Cook over medium heat, stirring all the time, until the sauce thickens. Stir in the mushrooms and season to taste.

6 Turn out each mousse onto a serving plate. Spoon over a little sauce and serve the remainder separately. Garnish with a sprig of fresh tarragon and serve with boiled rice and leeks.

Tagliatelle with Sun-dried Tomatoes

Choose plain sun-dried tomatoes for this sauce, instead of those preserved in oil, as they will increase the fat content.

Serves 4

INGREDIENTS
1 garlic clove, crushed
1 celery stalk finely sliced
1 cup sun-dried tomatoes, finely chopped
scant ½ cup red wine
8 plum tomatoes
12 oz dried tagliatelle
salt and freshly ground black pepper

sun-dried tomatoes

celery   *tagliatelle*

plum tomatoes

NUTRITIONAL NOTES
PER SERVING:

CALORIES 357 **PROTEIN** 12.36 g
FAT 2.32 g **SATURATED FAT** 0.32 g
CARBOHYDRATE 72.55 g **FIBER** 5.09 g
ADDED SUGAR 0 **SODIUM** 0.09 g

1 Put the garlic, celery, sun-dried tomatoes and wine into a large saucepan. Gently cook for 15 minutes.

2 Plunge the plum tomatoes into a saucepan of boiling water for 1 minute, then into a saucepan of cold water. Slip off their skins. Halve, remove the seeds and cores and roughly chop the flesh.

3 Add the plum tomatoes to the saucepan and simmer for a further 5 minutes. Season to taste.

4 Meanwhile, cook the tagliatelle in plenty of lightly salted rapidly boiling water for 8-10 minutes, or until *al dente*. Drain well. Toss with half the sauce and serve on warmed plates, topped with the remaining sauce.

Chili Bean Bake

The contrasting textures of spicy beans, vegetables and crunchy cornbread topping make this a memorable meal.

Serves 4

INGREDIENTS

1⅓ cups red kidney beans
1 bay leaf
1 large onion, finely chopped
1 garlic clove, crushed
2 celery stalks, sliced
1 tsp ground cumin
1 tsp chili powder
14 oz can chopped tomatoes
1 tbsp tomato paste
1 tsp dried mixed herbs
1 tbsp lemon juice
1 yellow bell pepper, seeded and diced
salt and freshly ground black pepper
mixed salad, to serve

FOR THE CORNBREAD TOPPING

1½ cups corn meal
1 tbsp whole wheat flour
1 tsp baking powder
1 egg, beaten
¾ cup skim milk

kidney beans

celery

tomato paste

pepper

NUTRITIONAL NOTES

PER SERVING:

CALORIES 399 **PROTEIN** 22.86 g
FAT 4.65 g **SATURATED FAT** 0.86 g
CARBOHYDRATE 70.86 g **FIBER** 11.59 g
ADDED SUGAR 0 **SODIUM** 0.72 g

1 Soak the beans overnight in cold water. Drain and rinse well. Pour 4 cups of water into a large, heavy-based saucepan together with the beans and bay leaf and boil rapidly for 10 minutes. Lower the heat, cover and simmer for 35–40 minutes, or until the beans are tender.

2 Add the onion, garlic clove, celery, cumin, chili powder, chopped tomatoes, tomato paste and dried mixed herbs. Half-cover the pan with a lid and simmer for a further 10 minutes.

3 Stir in the lemon juice, yellow pepper and seasoning. Simmer for a further 8-10 minutes, stirring occasionally, until the vegetables are just tender. Discard the bay leaf and spoon the mixture into a large casserole.

4 Preheat the oven to 425°F. For the topping, put the corn meal, flour, baking powder and a pinch of salt into a bowl and mix together. Make a well in the center and add the egg and milk. Mix and pour over the bean mixture. Bake in the preheated oven for 20 minutes, or until brown.

Ratatouille Crepes

These crepes are made slightly thicker than usual to hold the juicy vegetable filling.

Serves 4

INGREDIENTS
¾ cup flour
¼ cup oatmeal
1 egg
1¼ cups skim milk
mixed salad, to serve

FOR THE FILLING
1 large eggplant, cut into 1 in
    cubes
1 garlic clove, crushed
2 medium zucchini, sliced
1 green bell pepper, seeded and sliced
1 red bell pepper, seeded and sliced
5 tbsp vegetable stock
7 oz can chopped tomatoes
1 tsp cornstarch
salt and freshly ground black pepper

zucchini

oatmeal

pepper

cornstarch

chopped tomatoes

eggplant

flour   egg

1 Sift the flour and a pinch of salt into a bowl. Stir in the oatmeal. Make a well in the center, add the egg and half the milk and mix to a smooth batter. Gradually beat in the remaining milk. Cover the bowl and leave to stand for 30 minutes.

2 Spray a 7 in crepe pan or heavy-based frying pan with non-stick cooking spray. Heat the pan, then pour in just enough batter to cover the base of the pan thinly. Cook for 2-3 minutes, until the underside is golden brown. Flip over and cook for a further 1-2 minutes.

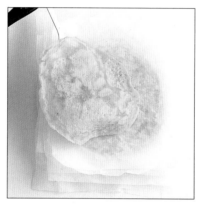

3 Slide the crepe out onto a plate lined with non-stick baking paper. Stack the other crepes on top as they are made, interleaving each with non-stick baking paper. Keep warm.

4 For the filling, put the eggplant in a colander and sprinkle well with salt. Leave to stand on a plate for 30 minutes. Rinse thoroughly and drain well.

5 Put the garlic clove, zucchini, peppers, stock and tomatoes into a large saucepan. Simmer uncovered and stir occasionally for 10 minutes. Add the eggplant and cook for a further 15 minutes. Blend the cornstarch with 2 tsp water and add to the saucepan. Simmer for 2 minutes. Season to taste.

NUTRITIONAL NOTES

PER SERVING:

CALORIES 182 **PROTEIN** 9.36 g
FAT 3.07 g **SATURATED FAT** 0.62 g
CARBOHYDRATE 31.40 g **FIBER** 4.73 g
ADDED SUGAR 0 **SODIUM** 0.22 g

6 Spoon the ratatouille mixture into the middle of each crepe. Fold each one in half, then in half again to make a cone shape. Serve hot with a mixed salad.

Vegetable Biryani

This exotic dish made from everyday ingredients will be appreciated by vegetarians and meat-eaters alike.

Serves 4–6

NUTRITIONAL NOTES
Per serving:

CALORIES 175 PROTEIN 3.66 g
FAT 0.78 g SATURATED FAT 0.12 g
CARBOHYDRATE 41.03 g FIBER 0.58 g
ADDED SUGAR 0 SODIUM 0.02 g

INGREDIENTS
1 cup long grain rice
2 whole cloves
seeds of 2 cardamom pods
scant 2 cups vegetable
    stock
2 garlic cloves
1 small onion, coarsely chopped
1 tsp cumin seeds
1 tsp ground cilantro
½ tsp ground turmeric
½ tsp chili powder
1 large potato, peeled and cut into
    1 in cubes
2 carrots, sliced
½ cauliflower, broken into florets
2 oz green beans, cut into
    1 in lengths
2 tbsp chopped fresh cilantro
2 tbsp lime juice
salt and freshly ground black pepper
sprig of fresh cilantro, to garnish

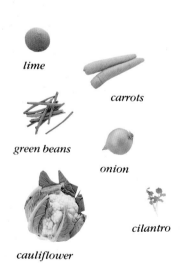

lime

carrots

green beans

onion

cilantro

cauliflower

1 Put the rice, cloves and cardamom seeds into a large, heavy-based saucepan. Pour over the stock and bring to a boil.

2 Reduce the heat, cover and simmer for 20 minutes, or until all the stock has been absorbed.

3 Meanwhile put the garlic cloves, onion, cumin seeds, cilantro, turmeric, chili powder and seasoning into a blender or food processor together with 2 tbsp water. Blend to a paste.

4 Preheat the oven to 350°F. Spoon the spicy paste into a flameproof casserole and cook over a low heat for 2 minutes, stirring occasionally.

5 Add the potato, carrots, cauliflower, beans and 6 tbsp water. Cover and cook over a low heat for a further 12 minutes, stirring occasionally. Add the chopped cilantro.

6 Spoon the rice over the vegetables. Sprinkle over the lime juice. Cover and cook in the oven for 25 minutes, or until the vegetables are tender. Fluff up the rice with a fork before serving and garnish with a sprig of fresh cilantro.

Herbed Baked Tomatoes

Dress up sliced, sweet tomatoes with fresh herbs and a crisp bread crumb topping.

Serves 4–6

INGREDIENTS
1½ lb (about 8) large red and yellow
 tomatoes
2 tsp red wine vinegar
½ tsp whole grain mustard
1 garlic clove, crushed
2 tsp chopped fresh parsley
2 tsp snipped fresh chives
½ cup fresh fine white bread
 crumbs
salt and freshly ground black pepper
sprigs of Italian parsley, to garnish

parsley

chives

tomatoes

mustard

vinegar

bread crumbs

NUTRITIONAL NOTES

Per serving:

CALORIES 47 **PROTEIN** 1.97 g
FAT 0.73 g **SATURATED FAT** 0.08 g
CARBOHYDRATE 8.63 g **FIBER** 1.98 g
ADDED SUGAR 0 **SODIUM** 0.15 g

1 Preheat the oven to 400°F. Thickly slice the tomatoes and arrange half of them in a 3¾ cup ovenproof dish, overlapping the slices.

2 Mix the vinegar, mustard, garlic clove and seasoning together. Stir in 2 tsp of cold water. Sprinkle the tomatoes with half the parsley and chives, then drizzle over half the dressing.

3 Lay the remaining tomato slices on top, overlapping them slightly. Drizzle with the remaining dressing.

4 Sprinkle over the bread crumbs. Bake in the preheated oven for 25 minutes or until the topping is golden. Sprinkle with the remaining parsley and chives. Serve immediately garnished with sprigs of Italian parsley.

Zucchini in Citrus Sauce

If baby zucchini are unavailable, you can use larger ones, but they should be cooked whole so that they don't absorb too much water. Halve them lengthwise and cut into 4 in lengths.

Serves 4

INGREDIENTS
12 oz baby zucchini
4 scallions, finely sliced
1 in fresh ginger root, grated
2 tbsp cider vinegar
1 tbsp light soy sauce
1 tsp soft light brown sugar
3 tbsp vegetable stock
finely grated rind and juice of ½
    lemon and ½ orange
1 tsp cornstarch

orange

lemon

zucchini

ginger

scallions

NUTRITIONAL NOTES
Per serving:

CALORIES 33 **PROTEIN** 2.18 g
FAT 0.42 g **SATURATED FAT** 0.09 g
CARBOHYDRATE 5.33 g **FIBER** 0.92 g
ADDED SUGAR 1.31 g **SODIUM** 0.55 g

1 Cook the zucchini in lightly salted boiling water for 3-4 minutes, or until just tender. Drain well.

2 Meanwhile put all the remaining ingredients, except the cornstarch, into a small saucepan and bring to a boil. Simmer for 3 minutes.

3 Blend the cornstarch with 2 tsp of cold water and add to the sauce. Bring to a boil, stirring continuously, until the sauce has thickened.

4 Pour the sauce over the zucchini and gently heat, shaking the pan to coat evenly. Transfer to a warmed serving dish and serve.

Mixed Mushroom Ragu

These mushrooms are delicious served hot or cold
and can be made up to two days in advance.

Serves 4

NUTRITIONAL NOTES

PER SERVING:

CALORIES 41 **PROTEIN** 2.51 g
FAT 0.66 g **SATURATED FAT** 0.08 g
CARBOHYDRATE 5.70 g **FIBER** 1.02 g
ADDED SUGAR 2.64 g **SODIUM** 0.63 g

INGREDIENTS

1 small onion, finely chopped
1 garlic clove, crushed
1 tsp cilantro seeds, crushed
2 tbsp red wine vinegar
1 tbsp soy sauce
1 tbsp dry sherry
2 tsp tomato paste
2 tsp light brown sugar
⅔ cup vegetable stock
4 oz baby button mushrooms
4 oz cremini mushrooms, quartered
4 oz oyster mushrooms, sliced
salt and freshly ground black pepper
sprig of fresh cilantro, to garnish

oyster mushrooms

sherry

cremini mushrooms

soy sauce

vinegar   *cilantro seeds*

tomato paste   *garlic*

cilantro

*button
mushrooms*

onion

1 Put the first nine ingredients into a large saucepan. Bring to a boil and reduce the heat. Cover and simmer for 5 minutes.

2 Uncover the saucepan and simmer for 5 more minutes, or until the liquid has reduced by half.

3 Add the baby button and cremini mushrooms and simmer for 3 minutes. Stir in the oyster mushrooms and cook for a further 2 minutes.

4 Remove the mushrooms with a slotted spoon and transfer them to a serving dish.

5 Boil the juices for about 5 minutes, or until reduced to about 5 tbsp. Season well with salt and pepper.

6 Allow to cool for 2-3 minutes, then pour over the mushrooms. Serve hot or well chilled, garnished with fresh cilantro.

Bulgur and Mint Salad with Fresh Vegetables

Also known as cracked wheat, burghul or pourgouri, the bulgur has been partially cooked, so it requires only a short soaking before serving.

Serves 4

INGREDIENTS

1⅔ cups bulgur
4 tomatoes
4 small zucchini, thinly sliced
   lengthwise
4 scallions, sliced on the diagonal
8 ready-to-eat dried apricots, chopped
¼ cup raisins
juice of 1 lemon
2 tbsp tomato juice
3 tbsp chopped fresh mint
1 garlic clove, crushed
salt and freshly ground black pepper
sprig of fresh mint, to garnish

zucchini *bulgur*

tomatoes

lemon

scallions

NUTRITIONAL NOTES

PER SERVING:

CALORIES 293 PROTEIN 8.72 g
FAT 1.69 g SATURATED FAT 0.28 g
CARBOHYDRATE 62.64 g FIBER 2.25 g
ADDED SUGAR 0.24 g SODIUM 0.09 g

1 Put the bulgur into a large bowl. Add enough cold water to come 1 in above the level of the wheat. Leave the bulgur to soak for 30 minutes, then drain well and squeeze out any excess water in a clean dish towel.

2 Meanwhile plunge the tomatoes into boiling water for 1 minute and then into cold water. Slip off the skins. Halve, remove the seeds and cores and roughly chop the flesh.

3 Stir the chopped tomatoes, sliced zucchini, scallions, apricots, and raisins into the bulgur.

4 Put the lemon and tomato juice, mint, garlic clove and seasoning into a small bowl and whisk together with a fork. Pour over the salad and mix well. Chill in the refrigerator for at least 1 hour. Serve garnished with a sprig of mint.

Vegetables à la Greque

This simple salad is made with winter vegetables, but you can vary it according to the season.

Serves 4

INGREDIENTS
¾ cup white wine
1 tsp olive oil
2 tbsp lemon juice
2 bay leaves
sprig of fresh thyme
4 juniper berries
1 lb leeks, trimmed and cut into 1 in
    lengths
1 small cauliflower, broken into
    florets
4 celery stalks, sliced on the diagonal
2 tbsp chopped fresh parsley
salt and freshly ground black pepper

wine

celery

cauliflower

parsley

olive oil

leeks

NUTRITIONAL NOTES
PER SERVING:

CALORIES 88 **PROTEIN** 4.53 g
FAT 2.05 g **SATURATED FAT** 0.11 g
CARBOHYDRATE 6.16 g **FIBER** 4.42 g
ADDED SUGAR 0 **SODIUM** 0.11 g

1 Put the wine, oil, lemon juice, bay leaves, thyme and juniper berries into a large, heavy-based saucepan and bring to a boil. Cover and leave to simmer for 20 minutes.

2 Add the leeks, cauliflower and celery. Simmer very gently for 5–6 minutes or until just tender.

COOK'S TIP
Choose a dry or medium-dry white wine for this dish.

3 Remove the vegetables with a slotted spoon and transfer them to a serving dish. Briskly boil the cooking liquid for 15-20 minutes, or until reduced by half. Strain.

4 Stir the parsley into the liquid and season to taste. Pour over the vegetables and leave to cool. Chill in the refrigerator for at least 1 hour before serving.

Fruit and Fiber Salad

Fresh, fast and filling, this salad makes a great starter, supper or snack.

Serves 4–6

INGREDIENTS

8 oz red or white cabbage or a
   mixture of both
3 medium carrots
1 pear
1 red-skinned apple
7 oz can lima beans,
   drained
¼ cup chopped dates

FOR THE DRESSING

½ tsp dry English mustard
2 tsp honey
2 tbsp orange juice
1 tsp white wine vinegar
½ tsp paprika
salt and freshly ground black pepper

carrot

dates

orange   lima
          beans

cabbage   pear   apple

1 Shred the cabbage very finely, discarding any tough stalks.

2 Cut the carrots into very thin strips, about 2 in long.

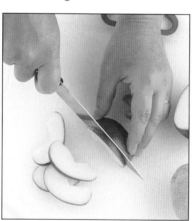

3 Quarter, core and slice the pear and apple, leaving the skin on.

4 Put the fruit and vegetables in a bowl with the beans and dates. Mix well.

5 For the dressing, blend the mustard with the honey until smooth. Add the orange juice, vinegar, paprika and seasoning and mix well.

NUTRITIONAL NOTES

PER SERVING:

CALORIES 137 **PROTEIN** 4.56 g
FAT 0.87 g **SATURATED FAT** 0.03 g
CARBOHYDRATE 29.43 g **FIBER** 6.28 g
ADDED SUGAR 1.91 g **SODIUM** 0.30 g

6 Pour the dressing over the salad and toss to coat. Chill in the refrigerator for 30 minutes before serving.

Potato Gratin

Don't rinse the potato slices before layering because the starch makes a thick sauce during cooking.

Serves 4

INGREDIENTS
1 garlic clove
5 large baking potatoes, unpeeled
3 tbsp freshly grated Parmesan cheese
2½ cups vegetable or low fat chicken stock
pinch of freshly grated nutmeg
salt and freshly ground black pepper

potatoes

Parmesan cheese

stock

NUTRITIONAL NOTES

PER SERVING:

CALORIES 221 PROTEIN 7.88 g
FAT 2.71 g SATURATED FAT 1.30 g
CARBOHYDRATE 43.77 g FIBER 3.30 g
ADDED SUGAR 0 SODIUM 0.21 g

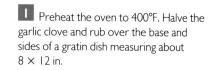

1 Preheat the oven to 400°F. Halve the garlic clove and rub over the base and sides of a gratin dish measuring about 8 × 12 in.

2 Slice the potatoes very thinly and arrange a third of them in the dish. Sprinkle with a little grated cheese, salt and freshly ground black pepper. Pour over some of the stock to prevent the potatoes from discoloring.

3 Continue layering the potatoes and cheese as before, then pour over the rest of the stock. Sprinkle with the nutmeg.

4 Bake in the oven for 1¼-1½ hours or until the potatoes are tender and the tops well browned.

VARIATION

For a potato and onion gratin, thinly slice one medium onion and layer with the potato.

Marinated Cucumber Salad

Sprinkling the cucumber with salt draws out some of the water and makes them crisper.

Serves 4–6

INGREDIENTS
2 medium cucumbers
1 tbsp salt
¼ cup sugar
¾ cup cider
1 tbsp cider vinegar
3 tbsp chopped fresh dill
pinch of pepper

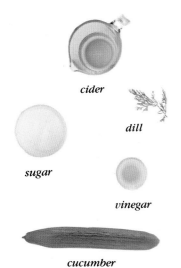

cider

dill

sugar

vinegar

cucumber

NUTRITIONAL NOTES

PER SERVING:

CALORIES 111 **PROTEIN** 0.52 g
FAT 0.14 g **SATURATED FAT** 0.01 g
CARBOHYDRATE 25.59 g **FIBER** 0.62 g
ADDED SUGAR 23.62 g **SODIUM** 0.02 g

1 Slice the cucumbers thinly and place them in a colander, sprinkling salt between each layer. Put the colander over a bowl and leave to drain for 1 hour.

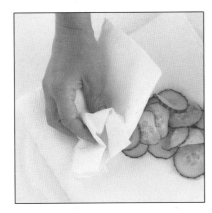

2 Thoroughly rinse the cucumber under cold running water to remove excess salt, then pat dry on absorbent paper towels.

3 Gently heat the sugar, cider and vinegar in a saucepan, until the sugar has dissolved. Remove from the heat and leave to cool. Put the cucumber slices in a bowl, pour over the cider mixture and leave to marinate for 2 hours.

4 Drain the cucumber and sprinkle with the dill and pepper to taste. Mix well and transfer to a serving dish. Chill in the refrigerator until ready to serve.

Apricot Delight

A fluffy mousse base with a layer of fruit jelly on top makes this dessert doubly delicious.

Serves 8

INGREDIENTS
2 × 14 oz cans apricots in natural juice
4 tbsp fructose
1 tbsp lemon juice
5 tsp powdered gelatin
15 oz low fat ready made custard
⅔ cup strained yogurt (see Introduction)
1 quantity yogurt piping cream (see Introduction), to decorate
1 apricot, sliced and sprig of fresh apple mint, to decorate

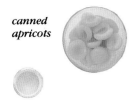

canned apricots

gelatin

custard

strained yogurt

NUTRITIONAL NOTES
PER SERVING:

CALORIES 155 **PROTEIN** 7.35 g
FAT 0.63 g **SATURATED FAT** 0.33 g
CARBOHYDRATE 31.89 g **FIBER** 0.90 g
ADDED SUGAR 3.53 g **SODIUM** 0.26 g

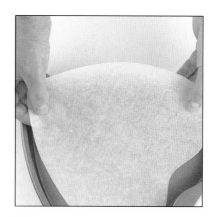

1 Line the base of a 5 cup heart-shaped cake pan with non-stick baking paper.

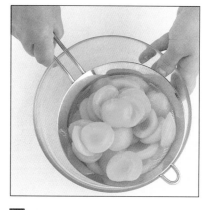

2 Drain the apricots, reserving the juice. Put the drained apricots in a food processor or blender fitted with a metal blade together with the fructose and 4 tbsp of the apricot juice. Blend to a smooth purée.

3 Measure 2 tbsp of the apricot juice into a small bowl. Add the lemon juice, then sprinkle over 2 tsp of the gelatin. Leave for about 5 minutes, until 'spongy'.

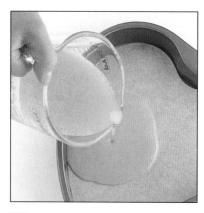

4 Stir the gelatin into half of the purée and pour into the prepared pan. Chill in a refrigerator for 1½ hours, or until firm.

COOK'S TIP
Don't use a loose-bottomed cake pan for this recipe as the mixture may seep through before it sets.

5 Sprinkle the remaining 1 tbsp of gelatin over 4 tbsp of the apricot juice. Soak and dissolve as before. Mix the remaining apricot purée with the custard, yogurt and gelatine. Pour onto the layer of set fruit purée and chill in the refrigerator for 3 hours.

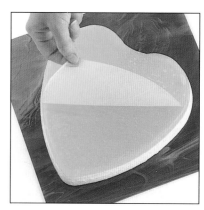

6 Dip the cake pan into hot water for a few seconds and unmold the delice onto a serving plate. Decorate with yogurt piping cream, the sliced apricot and sprigs of fresh apple mint.

Watermelon Sorbet

A slice of this refreshing sorbet is the perfect way to cool down on a hot sunny day.

Serves 4–6

INGREDIENTS
½ small watermelon, weighing about
  2¼ lb
½ cup superfine sugar
4 tbsp cranberry juice or water
2 tbsp lemon juice
sprigs of fresh mint, to decorate

cranberry juice

sugar

watermelon   lemon juice

NUTRITIONAL NOTES

PER SERVING:

CALORIES 125 PROTEIN 0.79 g
FAT 0.52 g SATURATED FAT 0
CARBOHYDRATE 31.29 g FIBER 0.26 g
ADDED SUGAR 19.69 g SODIUM 0.01 g

1 Cut the watermelon into 4–6 equal-sized wedges (depending on the number of servings you require). Scoop out the pink flesh, discarding the seeds but reserving the shell.

2 Line a freezer-proof bowl, about the same size as the melon, with plastic wrap. Arrange the melon skins in the bowl to re-form the shell, fitting them together snugly so that there are no gaps. Put in the freezer.

3 Put the sugar and cranberry juice or water in a saucepan and stir over a low heat until the sugar dissolves. Bring to a boil and simmer for 5 minutes. Leave the sugar syrup to cool.

4 Put the melon flesh and lemon juice in a blender and process to a smooth purée. Stir in the sugar syrup and pour into a freezer-proof container. Freeze for 3–3½ hours, or until slushy.

5 Tip the sorbet into a chilled bowl and whisk to break up the ice crystals. Return to the freezer for another 30 minutes, whisk again, then tip into the melon shell and freeze until solid.

6 Remove from the freezer and leave to defrost at room temperature for 15 minutes. Take the melon out of the bowl and cut into wedges with a warmed sharp knife. Serve with sprigs of fresh mint.

COOK'S TIP
If preferred, this pretty pink sorbet can be served scooped into balls. Do this before the mixture is completely frozen and re-freeze the balls on a baking sheet, ready to serve.

Feather-light Peach Pudding

On chilly days, try this hot fruit pudding with its tantalizing sponge topping.

Serves 4

INGREDIENTS

14 oz can peach slices in
 natural juice
4 tbsp low fat spread
¼ cup light brown sugar
1 egg, beaten
½ cup plain whole wheat
 flour
½ cup flour
1 tsp baking powder
½ tsp ground cinnamon
4 tbsp skim milk
½ tsp vanilla extract
2 tsp confectioner's sugar, for
 dusting
low fat ready-made custard,
 to serve

peach slices

flour

*confectioner's
sugar*

egg

brown sugar

*low fat
custard*

NUTRITIONAL NOTES

Per serving:

CALORIES 255 **PROTEIN** 6.49 g
FAT 6.78 g **SATURATED FAT** 1.57 g
CARBOHYDRATE 44.70 g **FIBER** 2.65 g
ADDED SUGAR 13.34 g **SODIUM** 0.70 g

1 Preheat the oven to 350°F. Drain the peaches and put into a 4 cup pie dish with 2 tbsp of the juice.

2 Put all the remaining ingredients, except the confectioner's sugar into a mixing bowl. Beat for 3–4 minutes, until thoroughly combined.

COOK'S TIP

For a simple sauce, blend 1 tsp arrowroot with 1 tbsp peach juice in a small saucepan. Stir in the remaining peach juice from the can and bring to a boil. Simmer for 1 minute until thickened and clear.

3 Spoon the sponge mixture over the peaches and level the top evenly. Cook in the oven for 35-40 minutes, or until springy to the touch.

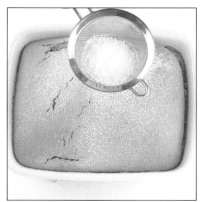

4 Lightly dust the top with confectioner's sugar and serve hot with the low fat custard.

Plum, Rum and Raisin Brulée

Crack through the crunchy caramel to find the juicy plums and smooth creamy center of this dessert.

Serves 4

INGREDIENTS

3 tbsp raisins
1 tbsp dark rum
12 oz medium plums (about 6)
juice of 1 orange
1 tbsp honey
2 cups low fat cream cheese
½ cup sugar

raisins

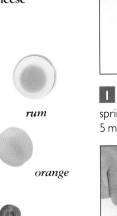

rum

orange

plums

honey

NUTRITIONAL NOTES

PER SERVING:

CALORIES 264 **PROTEIN** 5.71 g
FAT 8.56 g **SATURATED FAT** 5.11 g
CARBOHYDRATE 41.43 g **FIBER** 1.45 g
ADDED SUGAR 26.49 g **SODIUM** 0.66 g

1 Put the raisins into a small bowl and sprinkle over the rum. Leave to soak for 5 minutes.

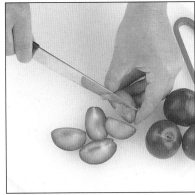

2 Quarter the plums and remove their pits. Put into a large, heavy-based saucepan together with the orange juice and honey. Simmer gently for 5 minutes or until soft. Stir in the soaked raisins. Reserve 1 tbsp of the juice, then divide the rest between four ⅔ cup ramekin dishes.

3 Blend the low fat cream cheese with the reserved 1 tbsp of plum juice. Spoon over the plums and chill in the refrigerator for 1 hour.

4 Put the sugar into a large, heavy-based saucepan with 3 tbsp cold water. Heat gently, stirring, until the sugar has dissolved. Boil for 15 minutes or until it turns golden brown. Cool for 2 minutes, then carefully pour over the ramekins. Cool and serve.

Red Fruit Fool

Frozen soft fruit is available in most supermarkets, making this a year-round treat.

Serves 4

INGREDIENTS
1 lb mixed red fruit, such as
    raspberries, red currants and
    strawberries
2 tsp fructose
½ tsp arrowroot
⅔ cup low fat whipping
    cream
1 tsp vanilla extract
fresh fruit, to decorate

strawberries

red currants

raspberries

1   Put the fruit and fructose into a large heavy-based saucepan and simmer over a low heat for 2 minutes, or until just soft.

2   Blend the arrowroot with 2 tsp cold water. Add to the fruit and simmer for a further minute, or until thickened. Cool and chill in the refrigerator for 1 hour.

3   Divide two-thirds of the fruit mixture between four individual glasses.

4   Purée the rest of the fruit and strain through a fine sieve to remove the seeds.

5   Lightly whip the cream and vanilla extract together until soft peaks form. Fold in the remaining fruit purée.

6   Spoon the fruit cream mixture between the glasses and chill for 30 minutes. Serve decorated with fresh fruit.

COOK'S TIP

Fructose is a natural fruit sugar. It is slightly sweeter than granulated sugar (sucrose) so less is needed. If you use granulated sugar instead, use 1 tbsp for this recipe.

NUTRITIONAL NOTES

PER SERVING:

CALORIES 105 **PROTEIN** 1.60 g
FAT 7.24 g **SATURATED FAT** 4.49 g
CARBOHYDRATE 8.88 g **FIBER** 1.31 g
ADDED SUGAR 1.31 g **SODIUM** 0.05 g

Blushing Pears

Pears poached in rosé wine and sweet spices absorb all the subtle flavors and turn a soft pink color.

Serves 6

INGREDIENTS
6 firm pears
1¼ cups rosé wine
⅔ cup cranberry or clear apple
  juice
strip of thinly pared orange rind
1 cinnamon stick
4 whole cloves
1 bay leaf
5 tbsp superfine sugar
small bay leaves, to decorate

wine

pears   *cranberry juice*

cinnamon

sugar

orange

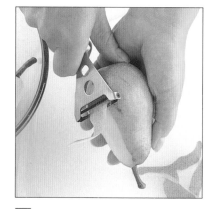

1 Thinly peel the pears with a sharp knife or vegetable peeler, leaving the stems attached.

2 Pour the wine and cranberry or apple juice into a large heavy-based saucepan. Add the orange rind, cinnamon stick, cloves, bay leaf and sugar.

3 Heat gently, stirring all the time until the sugar has dissolved. Add the pears and stand them upright in the pan. Pour in enough cold water to barely cover them. Cover and cook very gently for 20–30 minutes, or until just tender, turning and basting occasionally.

4 Using a slotted spoon, gently lift the pears out of the syrup and transfer to a serving dish.

5 Bring the syrup to a boil and boil rapidly for 10–15 minutes, or until it has reduced by half.

COOK'S TIP

Check the pears by piercing with a skewer or sharp knife towards the end of the poaching time because some may cook more quickly than others.

NUTRITIONAL NOTES

PER SERVING:

CALORIES 148 **PROTEIN** 0.48 g
FAT 0.16 g **SATURATED FAT** 0
CARBOHYDRATE 30.18 g **FIBER** 2.93 g
ADDED SUGAR 13.13 g **SODIUM** 0.02 g

6 Strain the syrup and pour over the pears. Serve hot or well-chilled, decorated with bay leaves.

Chocolate and Banana Brownies

Nuts traditionally give brownies their chewy texture. Here oat bran is used instead, creating a moist, tasty, yet healthy alternative.

Makes 9

INGREDIENTS

5 tbsp reduced fat cocoa powder
1 tbsp superfine sugar
5 tbsp skim milk
3 large bananas, mashed
1 cup light brown sugar
1 tsp vanilla extract
5 egg whites
¾ cup self-rising flour
¾ cup oat bran
1 tbsp confectioner's sugar, for dusting

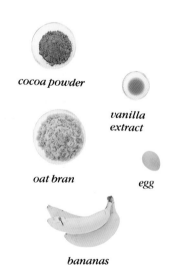

cocoa powder

vanilla extract

oat bran

egg

bananas

NUTRITIONAL NOTES

PER SERVING:

CALORIES 230 **PROTEIN** 5.24 g
FAT 2.15 g **SATURATED FAT** 0.91 g
CARBOHYDRATE 50.74 g **FIBER** 1.89 g
ADDED SUGAR 28.81 g **SODIUM** 0.32 g

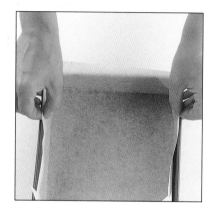

1 Preheat the oven to 350°F. Line a 8 in square pan with non-stick baking paper.

2 Blend the reduced fat cocoa powder and superfine sugar with the skim milk. Add the bananas, brown sugar and vanilla extract.

COOK'S TIP

Store these brownies in an airtight tin for a day before eating – they improve with keeping.

3 Lightly beat the egg whites with a fork. Add the chocolate mixture and continue to beat well. Sift the flour over the mixture and fold in with the oat bran. Pour into the prepared pan.

4 Cook in the preheated oven for 40 minutes or until firm. Cool in the pan for 10 minutes, then turn out onto a wire rack. Cut into 9 squares and lightly dust with confectioner's sugar before serving.

Cheese and Chive Scones

Feta cheese makes an excellent substitute for butter in these tangy savory scones.

Makes 9

INGREDIENTS
1 cup self-rising flour
1 cup self-rising whole wheat flour
½ tsp salt
3 oz feta cheese
1 tbsp snipped fresh chives
⅔ cup skim milk, plus extra for
   glazing
¼ tsp cayenne pepper

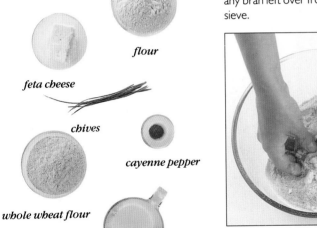

feta cheese

flour

chives

cayenne pepper

whole wheat flour

milk

1 Preheat the oven to 400°F. Sift the flours and salt into a mixing bowl, adding any bran left over from the flour in the sieve.

2 Crumble the feta cheese and rub into the dry ingredients. Stir in the chives, then add the milk and mix to a soft dough.

3 Turn out onto a floured surface and lightly knead until smooth. Roll out to ¾ in thick and stamp out nine scones with a 2½ in cookie cutter.

4 Transfer the scones to a non-stick baking sheet. Brush with skim milk, then sprinkle over the cayenne pepper. Bake in the oven for 15 minutes, or until golden brown. Serve warm or cold.

Carrot and Zucchini Cake

If you can't resist the lure of a slice of iced cake, you'll love this moist, spiced sponge cake with its delicious creamy topping.

Serves 10

INGREDIENTS
1 medium carrot
1 medium zucchini
3 eggs, separated
scant ½ cup light brown
   sugar
2 tbsp ground almonds
finely grated rind of 1 orange
1 cup self-rising whole wheat flour
1 tsp ground cinnamon
fondant carrots and zucchini, to
   decorate

FOR THE TOPPING
¾ cup low fat cream cheese
1 tsp honey

NUTRITIONAL NOTES
PER SERVING:

CALORIES 173 PROTEIN 6.25 g
FAT 6.31 g SATURATED FAT 2.22 g
CARBOHYDRATE 24.36 g FIBER 1.84 g
ADDED SUGAR 12.92 g SODIUM 0.26 g

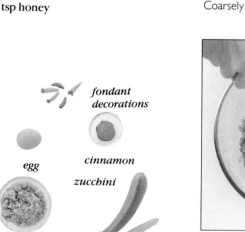

fondant decorations

egg   *cinnamon*

zucchini

brown sugar

carrot

orange

honey

1 Preheat the oven to 350°F. Line a 7 in square pan with non-stick baking paper. Coarsely grate the carrot and zucchini.

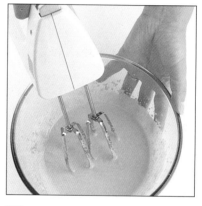

2 Put the egg yolks, sugar, ground almonds and orange rind into a bowl and whisk until very thick and light.

3 Sift together the flour and cinnamon and fold into the mixture together with the grated vegetables. Add any bran left over from the flour in the sieve.

4 Whisk the egg whites until stiff and carefully fold them in, a half at a time. Spoon into the prepared pan. Bake in the oven for 1 hour and cover the top with foil after 40 minutes.

5 Leave to cool in the tin for 5 minutes, then turn out onto a wire rack and carefully remove the lining paper.

6 For the topping, beat together the cheese and honey and spread over the cake. Decorate with fondant carrots and zucchini.

Chocolate and Orange Angel Cake

This light-as-air cake with its fluffy icing is virtually fat free, yet tastes heavenly.

Serves 10

INGREDIENTS
¼ cup flour
2 tbsp reduced fat cocoa powder
2 tbsp cornstarch
pinch of salt
5 egg whites
½ tsp cream of tartar
scant ½ cup superfine sugar
blanched and shredded rind of 1
 orange, to decorate

ICING
1 cup superfine sugar
1 egg white

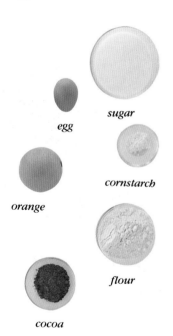

sugar

egg

cornstarch

orange

flour

cocoa

1 Preheat the oven to 350°F. Sift the flour, cocoa powder, cornstarch and salt together three times. Beat the egg whites in a large bowl until foamy. Add the cream of tartar, then whisk until soft peaks form.

2 Add the superfine sugar to the egg whites a spoonful at a time, whisking after each addition. Sift a third of the flour and cocoa mixture over the meringue and gently fold in. Repeat, sifting and folding in the flour and cocoa mixture two more times.

3 Spoon the mixture into a non-stick 8 in ring mold and level the top. Bake in the oven for 35 minutes or until springy when lightly pressed. Turn upsidedown onto a wire rack and leave to cool in the tin. Carefully ease out of the pan.

4 For the icing, put the sugar in a pan with 5 tbsp cold water. Stir over a low heat until dissolved. Boil until the syrup reaches a temperature of 240°F on a sugar thermometer, or when a drop of the syrup makes a soft ball when dropped into a cup of cold water. Remove from the heat.

5 Whisk the egg white until stiff. Add the syrup in a thin stream, whisking all the time. Continue to whisk until the mixture is very thick and fluffy.

NUTRITIONAL NOTES

PER SERVING:

CALORIES 153 **PROTEIN** 2.27 g
FAT 0.27 g **SATURATED FAT** 0.13 g
CARBOHYDRATE 37.79 g **FIBER** 0.25 g
ADDED SUGAR 34.65 g **SODIUM** 0.25 g

COOK'S TIP

Make sure you do not over-beat the egg whites. They should not be stiff but should form soft peaks, so that the air bubbles can expand further during cooking and help the cake to rise.

6 Spread the icing over the top and sides of the cooled cake. Sprinkle the orange rind over the top of the cake and serve.

INDEX

ACKNOWLEDGEMENTS

The author and publishers would like to thank Wendy Doyle of the Mother and Baby Clinic, London E9 for compiling the nutritional information for each recipe.